JIMI HENDRIX LONDON

William Saunders

MusicPlace Series

ROARING FORTIES
PRESS

Roaring Forties Press
1053 Santa Fe Avenue
Berkeley, California, 94706

ISBN 978-0-9843165-1-9

Library of Congress Cataloging-in-Publication Data
Saunders, William, 1958-
  Jimi Hendrix : London / William Saunders.
      p. cm. -- (MusicPlace series)
  Includes bibliographical references.
  ISBN 978-0-9843165-1-9 (pbk. : alk. paper) -- ISBN 978-0-9843165-2-6 (pdf)
-- ISBN 978-0-9843165-3-3 (epub) -- ISBN 978-0-9843165-4-0 (kindle)
  1. Hendrix, Jimi--Travel--England--London. 2. Rock musicians--Travel--England--
London. 3. London (England)--Description and travel. I. Title.
  ML410.H476S28 2010
  787.87166092--dc22
  [B]
                                                        2010031865

contents

acknowledgments

Thanks to Nigel and Deirdre for discovering the book I had always meant to write and for persisting until I did. While all sources are noted, I was grateful for conversations with John Hoppy Hopkins, Valerie Wilmer, and Joan Hills for background information. Thanks to Jon at Redferns for passing on enquiries to photographers from the era.

Thanks to Oisin Little for many long hours of instructive conversation on the art of guitar playing, long ago.

Thanks to Kate, Charlotte, and Felix, who have had the windows rattled by the Experience during the course of my research. And thanks to Jimi Hendrix, who is still remembered with a smile whenever his name comes up in London.

central london (west)

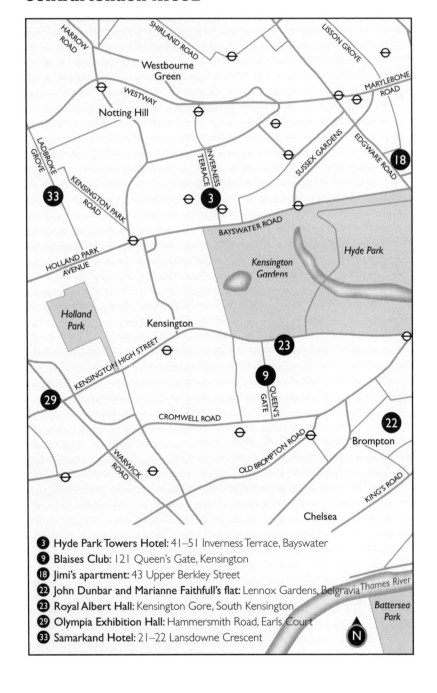

3 **Hyde Park Towers Hotel:** 41–51 Inverness Terrace, Bayswater
9 **Blaises Club:** 121 Queen's Gate, Kensington
18 **Jimi's apartment:** 43 Upper Berkley Street
22 **John Dunbar and Marianne Faithfull's flat:** Lennox Gardens, Belgravia
23 **Royal Albert Hall:** Kensington Gore, South Kensington
29 **Olympia Exhibition Hall:** Hammersmith Road, Earls Court
33 **Samarkand Hotel:** 21–22 Lansdowne Crescent

central london (east)

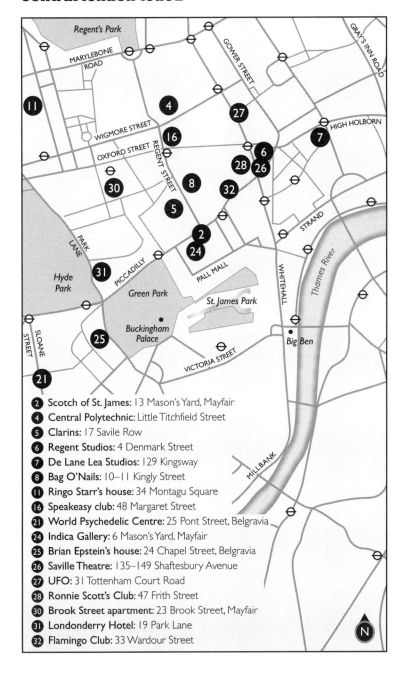

2 **Scotch of St. James:** 13 Mason's Yard, Mayfair
4 **Central Polytechnic:** Little Titchfield Street
5 **Clarins:** 17 Savile Row
6 **Regent Studios:** 4 Denmark Street
7 **De Lane Lea Studios:** 129 Kingsway
8 **Bag O'Nails:** 10–11 Kingly Street
11 **Ringo Starr's house:** 34 Montagu Square
16 **Speakeasy club:** 48 Margaret Street
21 **World Psychedelic Centre:** 25 Pont Street, Belgravia
24 **Indica Gallery:** 6 Mason's Yard, Mayfair
25 **Brian Epstein's house:** 24 Chapel Street, Belgravia
26 **Saville Theatre:** 135–149 Shaftesbury Avenue
27 **UFO:** 31 Tottenham Court Road
28 **Ronnie Scott's Club:** 47 Frith Street
30 **Brook Street apartment:** 23 Brook Street, Mayfair
31 **Londonderry Hotel:** 19 Park Lane
32 **Flamingo Club:** 33 Wardour Street

the london area

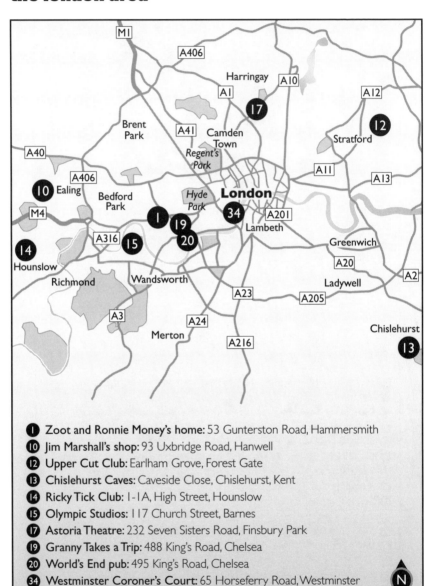

1. **Zoot and Ronnie Money's home:** 53 Gunterston Road, Hammersmith
10. **Jim Marshall's shop:** 93 Uxbridge Road, Hanwell
12. **Upper Cut Club:** Earlham Grove, Forest Gate
13. **Chislehurst Caves:** Caveside Close, Chislehurst, Kent
14. **Ricky Tick Club:** 1-1A, High Street, Hounslow
15. **Olympic Studios:** 117 Church Street, Barnes
17. **Astoria Theatre:** 232 Seven Sisters Road, Finsbury Park
19. **Granny Takes a Trip:** 488 King's Road, Chelsea
20. **World's End pub:** 495 King's Road, Chelsea
34. **Westminster Coroner's Court:** 65 Horseferry Road, Westminster

JIMI
HENDRIX
LONDON

Whether hem lines rose or fell, knee-high leather boots were a fashion essential in Swinging London. Four models pose to advertise the opening of a boutique on Chelsea's King's Road in 1967.

when london swung

Like several districts in London, World's End takes its name from a pub beside which the buses stop. In 1980 it seemed an apt name for the streets at the ugly end of Chelsea dominated by decrepit Victorian buildings that housed small factories and antique warehouses.

Schoolkids would pass a joint around as we played the Space Invaders machine in the corner shop just down the road from the World's End pub. Across the road from the pub itself was a greengrocer's run by a tiny man who wore a little peaked cap and a black beard down to his chest and who was always accompanied by a scrawny dog. On rainy days this shop had an awning that came down to protect the fruit and vegetables stacked on the sidewalk. The awning was a dazzling lemon yellow, with a drawing of a witchy woman's face painted in pale green and, written beneath her in red lettering, the words "Granny Takes a Trip."

The awning, which had once belonged to a trendy boutique of the same name, was a relic of the Summer of Love. It seemed to me like a messenger from a lost world. Thirteen years after it had passed, that summer was both enshrined in legend and the subject of debate. On one side of the debate were those who approved of the many social changes that had come about in the 1960s and questioned whether they had gone far enough. On the other side stood those who had disapproved of them and feared that they would be the cause of imminent social breakdown.

The World's End pub stands at the western end of the long King's Road. Local folklore claims that the road was built by King Charles II over three hundred years ago so he could visit his mistress, the actress Nell Gywnne, in what was then her country home. There is no historical doubt that Nell Gwynne, one of the most popular Londoners who ever lived, persuaded Charles to found the Chelsea Hospital, a convalescent and retirement home for veteran soldiers at the eastern end of King's Road. The scarlet-coated old veterans are a popular subject of picture postcards.

Elsewhere on the King's Road are numerous boutiques catering to a younger crowd with a taste for far more extravagant attire. In 1980, at the beginning of the yuppie decade, the style was the frills and bows worn by the Sloane Rangers (who took their name from Sloane Square at the east of King's Road). It was a look that harked back in some ways to the 1950s, and reflected a general view that the 1960s, for better or worse, were over and done with. It was also a look that aspired to appear aristocratic. The most famous Sloane Ranger was Diana Spencer, who would become Princess of Wales when she married Prince Charles.

Aged twenty in 1980 and on the run from a privileged education, I was drawn to the dismal end of King's Road where the tattered rags of 1967 still fluttered. Yet thirteen years is not such a long time, and the friends I made around World's End whose own youth had coincided with the Summer of Love were barely into middle age. Working-class men, married with young children, the London they recalled was not a utopia of bright young things, and sometimes it sounded as squalid as anything to be found in the novels of Dickens. But they recalled the ease with which work was to be found, the extravagant dandyism, the shock of the arrival of LSD, and above all the music. Among the musicians they recalled was Jimi Hendrix, and they remembered him not as a stadium god but as a club performer: by far the best club performer but one of many of his kind, several of whom were pretty good in their own right.

In the early 1980s, kids like me were discovering Hendrix for the first time. He had been associated with progressive rock and the long—and, so it seemed to us, self-indulgent—instrumental solos. But the arrival of George Clinton's music with Parliament and Funkadelia caused us to listen to the musician Clinton claimed as his own inspiration. Seeing Jimi as a flesh-and-blood pioneer rather than an idealized historical figure made the thought of those club performances all the more intriguing. What a journey into the unknown they must have been, what a journey into the unknown that whole era was.

Some books about Jimi Hendrix promise "The Truth." I do not make such an audacious claim. I do hope that by putting him back into the time and place from which he emerged he will become a little more real, and that the artist that he was will emerge from the distortions of myths.

In 1966 Britishness was cool. At the end of April, *Time* magazine dedicated an issue to the claim that London was the world city that best embodied the spirit of the decade. Above all, London was the city of the young in the decade when youth set the style. Almost half the population was under thirty years old. And in London the young enjoyed unprecedented prosperity and independence, compared with their parents and grandparents and with many of their contemporaries elsewhere in the British Isles. Cheap rents made independent living easy and attractive. A bed-sitting-room, a furnished room in what had once been a large Victorian or Georgian family house, cost only a few pounds a week. Bed-sit living meant sharing a bathroom with half a dozen other people, and kitchen facilities might be no more than a hot plate on a staircase landing. These conditions were neither Spartan nor unhygienic by the standards of the time. Refrigerators were still a luxury, and thousands of London homes had no indoor bathroom at all. In any case, the young did not rent bed-sits so they could enjoy the comforts of home. The daytime was for working, and the nighttime was for clubs, coffee bars, and parties.

Rent accounted for about a third of a young person's income. Much of the rest was likely to be spent on clothes. The spending power of London's young influenced the world's fashions. Influence was wrenched from the couture houses of Paris by a generation of British designers who catered to the extravagance of London's *sans culottes*.

London was the original home of the miniskirt, launched by the designer Mary Quant and made possible by the invention of pantyhose and the tampon. John Stephen among others had radicalized men's fashions beginning in a West End Street that was little more than an alley behind Regent Street when he opened his first men's boutique there in 1958. Ten years later Carnaby Street was synonymous with Swinging London. Designers had to try to keep up with the creativity of their customers. Many young Londoners preferred to make individual style statements with vintage clothing bought from the market stalls of Portobello Road near Notting Hill.

And, in rather roundabout ways, London had become the center of a blues revival, which was one of the things that encouraged a young blues guitarist who worked under the name of Jimmy James to try his luck there.

chapter 1

just like a rolling stone

no direction home

Jimi Hendrix arrived at Heathrow Airport at 9 a.m. on September 24, 1966, a Saturday morning. He had set off from New York City under another name entirely. For the past year or so his professional name had been Jimmy James. The exotic spelling Jimi was decided on during the flight over the Atlantic.

Interviewed five years later, Jimi's manager Chas Chandler was not sure whether they had agreed to convert to Hendrix from Hendricks at the same time. In fact, although the origin of Jimi's surname probably is the English "Hendricks," his paternal ancestors had been using the spelling "Hendrix" for at least three generations. There had been much to talk about on the plane; the journey was a flight into the unknown for both young men.

Chas, twenty-eight years old to Jimi's twenty-three, with a career as bass player in an internationally successful pop group behind him, was the leader of the expedition. He was full of ideas but had little substance to back them up.

a woman's touch

Chas had made up his mind to bring Jimi to London as soon as he had heard him play. That had been in the Cafe Wha? in Greenwich Village, six weeks previously in early August, where Chas had been taken by Linda Keith, the person who has the best claim to have discovered Jimi Hendrix. Linda, a Londoner and a fashion model, had come to New York City to await the arrival of her boyfriend, Keith Richards. She had spotted Jimi in a nightclub playing guitar with R&B singer Curtis Knight, and been struck by his musicianship and his physical charisma. She had invited him first to her table and then to her hotel room, where they had sat up all night listening to Linda's collection of blues 78s and to Bob Dylan's newly released double album *Blonde on Blonde*. Jimi had been grateful for an occasion to unburden himself of his passion for Bob Dylan. Apart from his excursions to the Village, his base in NYC was Harlem, and his friends there had no interest in white pop music. The night was the beginning of an intense friendship, and Linda became Jimi's patron. Since he had arrived in NYC in 1964 Jimi had depended on female patronage for survival, but in Linda he found a patron with ambition and influence. She turned first to the Rolling Stones' manager, Andrew Loog Oldham, who came to listen but passed on the option. Then she ran into Chas.

Chas told her that his band, the Animals, were falling apart and that he planned to go into management. She took him to see Jimi play at the eccentric Café Wha? and introduced them during a break in the set. Chas's only doubt, as Jimi took the stage again after their introduction, was why Jimi had not been signed before. These doubts were blown away by an astonishing coincidence. Without knowing what kind of act he would discover as he turned to management, Chas had already determined that its first single would be "Hey Joe" (then a recent minor hit for the Leaves). Without any prompting, Jimi's first number of his second set was "Hey Joe." Through either destiny or serendipity, the Jimi Hendrix Experience had come into being.

a complete unknown

Jimi and Chas made a striking impression when they presented themselves at Immigration at Heathrow. Chas was six feet three inches tall, with a barrel chest, blond hair, and blue eyes. Before becoming a professional musician, he had worked as a docker in his native Newcastle and, an assertive man, he used his imposing physical presence to emphasize his point of view in any dispute. Jimi was the slighter but more conspicuous of the two. Five feet ten inches tall, he appeared much taller due to the explosion of hair piled on the top of his head, a highly idiosyncratic hairstyle he had devised and coiffed himself with the aid of Bayliss hair rollers, a homage to and an extraordinary imitation of Bob Dylan's loose white-afro curls. He was slender but big boned, as evidenced not only by the magnetic cheekbones that made him so photogenic but also by a pair of large, strong hands. The size of his feet was emphasized by boots with long pointed toes, which would have struck any fashion-conscious spectator as passé. Nobody would have known that the soles of Jimi's boots were worn through, and that in one of them there was a dollar bill concealed. Jimi had taken up the habit of always having a dollar that only he knew about after he had been left stranded when he missed a tour bus while traveling through the rural South as a sideman to one of the many R&B stars he worked for during his years of apprenticeship. The single bill had talismanic significance as well as practical use. Three years later, when he was the best-paid concert performer in the world, he still traveled with a dollar bill tucked into his hat band to ward off the poverty that had oppressed him all his life.

Jimi moved like a taller man than he was, too, with the incline of the head and shoulders known as a "scholar's stoop," and with a clumsy, uncoordinated gait that one might associate with an absent-minded professor. He was by the far the quieter of the two men, inclined to hang back, listen, or even appear uninvolved in what was going on around him. It was a manner often mistaken for shyness. But when drawn into conversation Jimi quickly revealed a playful geniality and a readiness for intimacy that women, and many men, found seductive. That geniality was to be tested on arrival at Heathrow because it took Chas and Jimi three hours to clear Customs.

the mystery tramp

The delay at Heathrow was due to doubts over Jimi's visa. There had not been time to apply for a full work permit, and getting the paperwork in order had taken longer than expected. But Chas had booked the flights and could not afford to cancel them, so Jimi entered the United Kingdom of Great Britain and Northern Ireland as a visitor; because he was traveling with barely enough luggage for a weekend's stay, the Immigration officials became suspicious. Their doubts were not allayed until Chas persuaded a publicist from the Animals' management company to come out to the airport and finesse Jimi through with a story that he was an American soul singer who had come to Britain to spend his UK royalties, a plausible tale in an era of tight foreign exchange controls and that also accounted for the fact that Jimi had only $40 with him.

the lost boy

The baby who would become Jimi Hendrix was born on November 27, 1942, in Seattle. His mother, Lucille, was seventeen years old and his father, Al, was away in the military. Lucille's unexpected pregnancy and Al's impending call up to serve in World War II had been the catalysts that had turned a dance hall romance into an unpromising marriage. Nevertheless, Al and Lucille's relationship was to hold together for as long as Lucille's short life lasted, through many stormy partings and one visit to the divorce court. That it did so was due to Al's determination to hold on to his son. Even with the support of an extended family, Lucille struggled with motherhood, and the infant Jimi was fostered to a family in California. Jimi was three years old, and on the point being adopted by his foster family, when Al, who had just been demobilized, arrived to reclaim him. Al took Jimi back to Seattle, where Al also reclaimed Lucille, who had formed another relationship while Al had been serving in the military.

Between 1948 and 1953, Al and Lucille had five more children together: Leon, Joe, Kathy, Pamela, and Alfred. The latter four were all born with such severe developmental difficulties that Lucille had no other realistic alternative than to put them in the care of the City of Seattle. Even in the 1950s it was suspected that these developmental difficulties were linked to Lucille's heavy drinking, a suspicion that added to Lucille's burden of guilt over her inadequacies as a mother.

Al's mother was a full-blooded Cherokee; Lucille's family roots were in Tennessee and Arkansas, and it is very likely that she too had Native American ancestry. Always as indifferent to race as society allowed him to be, when asked to identify himself, Jimi Hendrix considered himself to be Cherokee rather than African American.

Lucille was a semi-detached presence in the family home. Al was the constant presence in his sons' lives, and, torn between being both provider and parent, his household was usually both chaotic and impoverished. The Hendrix boys depended on the generosity of neighbors for such basic needs as regular meals. Lucille's tarantella of a life ended in February 1958, when she died, alone, in hospital of a ruptured spleen brought on by a fall. She was thirty-two years old, five years older than her eldest son would be when he died, and already suffering from hepatitis and cirrhosis of the liver. Jimi Hendrix was fifteen. Even before kindergarten he had been noted as a child of inner resources, and his mother's death pushed him further into his own imagination and bequeathed to him a reckless disregard for the future.

the wild man of borneo

Once clear of Immigration, Chas's first move was to plunge Jimi into London's music scene. To this end he diverted the taxi from the main route into London, to **(1) 53 Gunterston Road, Hammersmith.** All that most first-time visitors to London see of

Hammersmith is its grey slate roofs, as the elevated motorway from Heathrow dips and dives through a complicated intersection and speeds them on to the center of the city. Hammersmith is a late-Victorian suburb, a maze of streets of terrace houses, each two or three stories high and fronting almost straight on to the sidewalk apart from a small yard with enough room for a couple of trash cans and grandiosely referred to as the "front garden." 53 Gunterston Road, as undistinguished as its neighbors, was the home of Zoot Money, a rumbustious bandleader, and his Scottish wife Ronnie. With Zoot's band already assembling for that evening's gig, the door was wide open to the two unexpected guests. Jimi, who loved to jam more than anything else, walked in, grabbed an unplugged electric guitar, and took the floor.

Upstairs twenty-year-old Kathy Etchingham was still asleep after a late night clubbing. A reluctant apprentice hairdresser by day, she had a reputation as a disc jockey by night. Ronnie Money went up to wake her, and told her that she must come down and see this amazing visitor who looked "like the Wild Man of Borneo" (an expression that referred to Jimi's hair, not his race). Kathy refused to stir, but sleepily she did agree to meet Ronnie, as well as Chas and his funny American friend, later on at the Scotch of St. James club.

a corny line and a catfight

For more than three hundred years, the St. James district has been the place where London's most influential citizens have met for leisure and gossip. It begins at Piccadilly Circus, famous for its huge electronic advertising displays, and follows a gentle slope down to the Mall, the long front drive of Buckingham Palace. St. James has always been a place of intrigue, where secrets have been swapped, alliances formed, and deals struck in intimate places of entertainment. Over the centuries, the nature of those places of entertainment has changed. In the early eighteenth century the district was the home of the London coffee houses, where young men gathered to show off their wit to one another. Later in that century it became the base of the dining clubs that formed around political factions and evolved into gentleman's clubs, where politicians and other men of influence could conspire. In the 1960s, London had a new, youthful elite, an ostensibly more democratic one, composed of television producers, pop stars, actors, and photographers, although it mingled closely with the children of the old elite. It was natural that this elite should convene where the London elite always has, and equally natural that St. James should offer it the entertainment it craved: the discotheque. The **(2) Scotch of St. James**, 13 Mason's Yard, Mayfair, was set in a secluded yard entered beneath an arch. Outrageously decorated with plaid to resemble a Scottish hunting lodge, the Scotch was a place where London's class barrier had become invisible, although it remained tangible enough for anyone who attempted to cross it without belonging to either the aristocratic or the artistic incrowd.

Whoever was playing at the Scotch, the background noise was usually a conspiratorial hum, so Kathy was surprised to find the audience silent when she caught up with Ronnie Money. Everyone was listening to a young man hunched over a guitar on stage.

The seed of Hendrix's success in London had been planted fifteen years earlier, when another African American guitarist had made his debut in London. In 1951 Big Bill Broonzy had played a solo concert at the Kingsway Hall. Interest in the blues was very limited at the time, and Broonzy drew an audience of around forty people to the large Methodist chapel. Knowledge of the blues was limited too, and probably none of the audience was aware that Broonzy was not a bluesman, at least not by the strictest standards.

Before World War II, Broonzy had enjoyed a prosperous musical career in Chicago as a bandleader, composer, and night-club proprietor. He had also been one of the pioneers of electric guitar. Left behind as a jazz musician by the emergence of bebop, he shrewdly acquired an acoustic guitar and began to see what "folk blues" could offer. The war had cut off British jazz musicians from the new developments that the music went through in the first half of the 1940s in the after-hours sessions in the clubs of New York City. When communications between British and American musicians were finally restored, the British were bewildered by the bebop sound created by musicians such as Charlie Parker, Dizzy Gillespie, and Bud Powell, as well as challenged by the virtuosity required to play it. The few British bebop enthusiasts were kept at arms length by the mainstream, which turned back to the jazz of the 1920s.

One of the early traditions of jazz that was revived in the London of the 1950s was "skiffle." Skiffle or "scuffle" was an African American word used to describe performances on homemade or cheap instruments, such as tin whistles and harmonicas. In London the word came to be used for performances during the intervals at jazz concerts that showcased the talents (or lack thereof) of the players such as guitarists and string bassists who were drowned out by brass players in full concert. Then a young man who called himself Lonnie Donegan made skiffle a household word throughout the British Isles.

In the mid 1950s he began to cut records loosely based on the style of Huddie Leadbetter, known as Leadbelly. Donegan took on Leadbetter's driving, powerful playing style but adapted his traditional material to be more comprehensible to British ears. For example, the old cocaine blues "Honey Take a Whiff on Me" became the far more gregarious "Come on Have Drink on Me." Loud but light-hearted, and somewhat reminiscent of the working-class music hall acts of the Victorian vaudeville, which was only just fading away, Donegan achieved what the jazz purists could not: he made the conservative BBC playlist, and as a result his records were massive hits.

His style was also very easy to imitate. Just as punk rock would do twenty years later, skiffle blurred the line between audience and performers, allowed enthusiasm to count for as much as skill, and put music-making into the hands of the young. By the late 1950s journalists would claim that half the young men and teenage boys in Britain were members of a skiffle band. John Lennon and Paul McCartney first met in a Liverpool schoolboy skiffle outfit called the Quarrymen.

In the Scotch of St. James that night, Jimi was playing something a lot more sophisticated than skiffle. As Kathy discovered, the crowd seemed enthralled—all except Chas, who was in a state of agitation. Even unpaid, Jimi's public performance was in violation of his tourist's visa. It was not long before Chas hustled Jimi off stage and introduced him to Kathy. She was immediately attracted to him. He seemed utterly outlandish, and at the same time gentle and sincere. When another young woman at the table went to the bathroom, Jimi took the opportunity to draw Kathy nearer to him. "I think you're beautiful," he whispered to her.

"It was a corny line," Kathy recalls in her memoirs, "but there was something sweet and innocent about the way he said it." She was disarmed and tried to disguise her feelings with small talk. Small talk became more difficult when the girl she had displaced returned and sat next to Ronnie. The atmosphere quickly soured, and then it erupted after the girl whispered something unpleasant about Kathy to Ronnie and Ronnie loudly took Kathy's side. The girl seized Ronnie's hair and Ronnie smashed a bottle on the table and threatened to push the jagged end into the girl's throat. Already nervous, Chas came close to panic at the prospect of the police being called. He thrust Jimi at Kathy and told her to take him to his hotel.

A motor scooter is parked outside the building that once housed the Scotch of St. James, where the Experience first performed in London.

On a street of tailors' shops, 17 Savile Row is woven into the tapestry of rock-and-roll history as the first place where the Experience rehearsed.

chapter 2

are you experienced?

another throw of the dice

The Wednesday morning of September 28, 1966, found Noel Redding on a train from the seaside resort of Hastings on the south coast of England. He was a scholarly looking boy of twenty, tall with wire spectacles resting on a long thin nose with a high bridge and a mad professor frizz of curls on top of his head. He was on his way to London to give his music career another throw of the dice.

Dressed casually in jeans on a weekday, he easily could have been mistaken for a college student. The copy of the *Melody Maker* he had in his hand would have reinforced that impression. It was a trade paper for the music industry, but its excellent standards of journalism and the sophistication of its jazz criticism brought it a much wider readership.

Noel was carrying the paper for its "Musicians Wanted" advertisements. He had abandoned his education four years earlier when he dropped out of art school with the ambition of becoming a professional guitarist. So far, however, he had known mostly the lows of musical life: broken-down vans on snowy nights, tens of miles from anywhere and hundreds of miles from home; long stints playing rock-and-roll covers to American servicemen in German clubs; and lately a record deal with the record label Pye that had faded to nothing through poor sales and a quarrel with his manager.

This morning his feelings were a mixture of resignation and reckless ambition. He had decided that competition was too tight among guitarists and that he should aim to become a drummer. Then, after buying the *Melody Maker*, he saw that a guitarist was required for Eric Burdon's new band and decided to take a shot at the big time.

After his train had pulled in to Charing Cross Station, Noel went to the Regent Street address given in the advertisement, stopped someone in the lobby and sold himself as best he could. He was directed to the auditions next day at a club in Soho called the Telephone Box. Soho is a network of backstreets in the heart of London. In those days, Soho was a cosmopolitan village where delicatessens stood next to striptease clubs, excellent French restaurants sat close to all-day drinking dens, and poets and artists mingled with streetwalkers and unlicensed bookies in the pubs.

When Noel reached the Telephone Box, the club seemed uncomfortably exposed with its lights full on, revealing graffiti-covered walls. Noel felt somewhat exposed himself. After four hard and fruitless years, he had gate-crashed into a dream-zone where the famous and unknown stood around bored, idle, and tense as the audition process ground on. He did his audition piece and although he received no reaction, felt sure he had not made the grade. He hung around, however, and found himself in conversation with Chas Chandler.

Before that morning the closest Noel had been to stardom was the time he had talked his way into the dressing room of the rock and roller Johnny Kidd as a teenager. Choosing his words carefully, Noel managed to give Chas the impression that he had toured with Kidd. Chas said that he was putting together a band for a guitarist who had just come over from America. Would Noel like to try out for bassist? Noel, who had never picked up a bass before, said yes.

Noel had already noticed Jimi as a mysterious figure hanging around in the background. In the short time he had been in London, Jimi had managed to acquire a classic Burberry trench-coat, which he wore indoors, buttoned up. The combination with Jimi's exotic perm was striking. Chas introduced them, and Jimi wasted no time in cross-examining Noel on his credentials. After introducing Noel to a drummer and a pianist, Jimi took Noel through the chords of "Hey Joe," which they played together for over an hour. Chas, watching them, saw that they had a good rapport. Both were young men who took life lightly and liked to see the funny side of things.

Chas was also struck that Noel, with his natural frizz and gawkiness, could be Jimi's white twin. At the end of the session he presented Noel with ten shillings for his travel expenses, and a chocolate bar, both welcome to a musician on the breadline, and invited him to come back the following day.

When the next day came, however, it appeared that the opportunity was about to join the list of Noel's other lost hopes. He had been told come to the Birdland club close to Piccadilly Circus, but when he arrived it was empty. He ran all the way along Chas's offices at 40 Gerrard Street. Inside he met a sharply dressed man and blurted out his troubles to him. The man asked Noel his name, and when he heard it, told him had nothing to worry about, he had the job. Noel had just met Mike Jeffries, the man he would come to consider the most malign influence on his life.

No aspect of Chandler's management of Hendrix has been questioned as much as his decision to go into partnership with Mike Jeffries. The man was so elusive that there was some confusion over his real name. He was born Michael Jeffrey but was known to everybody in the music business as Jeffries. That he never attempted to correct this would be appear to be due to a fundamental slipperiness of character.

Jeffries had been the Animals' manager, and it was due to Jeffries' divisive management, which had enriched some members of the band and left others with nothing, that Chandler needed financial support for his ambitions to become a manager himself, having learned the bitter lesson that in music it is the managers who make the money. Like the Animals, Jeffries was from Newcastle, but unlike the band he had been born into the upper middle class and enjoyed a privileged British public school (i.e., private school) education. From the end of World War II until the beginning of the 1960s all British young men were required to complete eighteen months military service. Jeffries' public school background eased him into an officer's commission, and he performed what was known as his National Service in Military Intelligence in Egypt. This intelligence background, together with the air of mystery Jeffries liked to cultivate, often evokes comparisons with James Bond. Sgt. Bilko appears to be a better comparison, because Jeffries spent his time in Egypt enriching himself through black market scams. On being honorably discharged, he went to Newcastle University and became head of entertainment for the Student Union. The experience of promoting concerts and the considerable proceeds of his Middle East adventures allowed him to go into the nightclub business in Newcastle, where he encountered the Animals and steered them to the top of not only the British but also the U.S. charts.

Dislike of Jeffries is not limited to those like Chandler and Eric Burdon who had reason to believe that he had swindled them. The American agency journalist Sharron Lawrence, who was a close friend of Hendrix, recalls that she would feel physically ill in Jeffries' presence. A more flattering portrait is painted by the British music journalist Norman Joplin, who met Jeffries in New York in the early 1970s and judged him to be a sincere believer in the values of the counterculture, far more excited by the artistic rather than the financial side of the music business. Jeffries also gave Joplin a much-needed loan, which turned out to be closer to a gift.

a toss of a coin

The Monday of the same week, Mitch Mitchell had been called into the management offices for Georgie Fame and the Blue

Flames and had learned that his services were no longer required as drummer. Mitch had no reason to be depressed over the loss of his job. An elfin-looking boy from the working-class west London suburb of Ealing, he was at twenty already a veteran of show business. A stage school pupil, he had been a child actor in the successful television series *Jennings*, in which he played a boy at an English boarding school. He had been a professional drummer, playing in bands and as a session player, since his teens. He owned his own car, an impressive achievement for a young Londoner not yet legally an adult.

Rumors of the shake-up of the Blue Flames lineup rippled out across Soho and reached Chas Chandler. That evening Chas telephoned Mitch and invited him to come down to the auditions. Mitch arrived the next day in a take-it-or-leave-it spirit. He had become frustrated with the repetitive life of touring, and had ambitions to stretch his musical talents. He spent a couple of hours jamming "In the Midnight Hour" with Jimi. Mitch knew the song—a hit for Wilson Pickett the year before—as a club standard, and Jimi had briefly been Pickett's guitarist.

There was no faulting Mitch's abilities, but Chas was indecisive. He had doubts about Mitch's cockiness. Mitch had all the mannerisms of a British actor of that time, including the fruity, slightly camp stage voice that was then standard among drama school graduates but that sounded grand and overbearing to people who were not used to actors. Kathy assumed he must be a member of the upper classes. Another drummer, Aynsley Dunbar, who had come to audition for Eric Burdon, had been equally impressive, and his journeyman background on the Northern club circuit was more comfortably familiar to Chas. The decision was made by tossing a coin in the taxi home. The coin came down in Mitch's favor.

house falling down

Home for Hendrix during his first months in London was the **(3) Hyde Park Towers Hotel**, 41–51 Inverness Terrace, a converted private house in a terrace of early nineteenth-century houses that runs north from Hyde Park in the district known as Bayswater.

In the autumn of 1966 the Hyde Park Towers Hotel was in a decrepit state. "The hotel had been having problems with dry rot," Kathy Echingham recalls in her memoirs. "The first we knew of it was when one of our bed legs went through the floor as I jumped on the bed. The management more or less evacuated us and closed down that part of the building, moving us to another floor at the back. As more and more rooms became dangerous and uninhabitable we had the place almost to ourselves, so the fact that the bathrooms had to be shared with other people didn't matter much. Most of the time, it was like living in a rather large and run-down private house."

gypsy eyes

Kathy moved in with Hendrix almost the day after she met him at the Scotch. Their ardent affair began when Kathy had seen Jimi back to his hotel. It was Kathy's first serious sexual relationship. Before Jimi, sex had been an extension of friendship for her, something that arose and then trailed off in the course of the close relationships she had formed first with Keith Moon, the drummer of the Who, and then with Brian Jones of the Rolling Stones.

The passionate foundation of Jimi's and Kathy's life together often broke to the surface in the form of loud and even violent quarrels in private and in public. Kathy was no stranger to turbulence, however, and the couple shared strong bonds that held them together.

Kathy's childhood had been almost as unsettled and uncertain as Jimi's own. She had been born just after the end of World War II in Derby, a town in the center of England that grew prosperous during the Industrial Revolution on the lead extracted from the bleak, granite moorland that surrounds it. Kathy's home life, for as long as it lasted, was more bleak than prosperous. The modest house into which she was born had no indoor bathroom, and the family bathed in a tin bath in front of the kitchen fire. This was not an unusual arrangement in the industrial towns of mid-twentieth-century Britain, but neither of her parents was emotionally equipped to seize the opportunities of the postwar boom. Her father was the dissolute son of an Anglo-Irish family whose fortunes had taken a turn for the worse during the Irish Civil War in the 1920s. He was not well prepared to earn a living, even without his tendency to alcoholic depression, so the family depended on the resourcefulness of Kathy's mother, Lil.

Lil was a restless, impatient, and frustrated woman of Gypsy descent, who began on motherhood in early middle age. Always looking to improve the family's finances, Lil decided to take in a young Irish laborer as a lodger. When Kathy was ten, Lil ran off with him. Kathy and her younger brother were sent to live with several eccentric relatives in Ireland before Kathy was placed as a permanent boarder at a convent school in Dublin. Just as she began to settle there, Lil reappeared and swept her away back to England to live.

Kathy made several attempts to run away to London during her teenage years, until at sixteen years old, she was legally of age to leave home and the authorities could not force her to return. In her early years in London she supported herself by waitressing in fast food restaurants and lived in bed-sit land. One night, at a party in St. John's Wood, near Regent's Park Zoo, she struck up a lasting friendship with another teenage girl, Angela King. Angie was the girlfriend of Eric Burdon and introduced Kathy to the inner circle of London's music scene. Jimi arrived in London with the musical talent to place himself at the center of London's rock world but without the social skills to get himself accepted by rock's aristocracy. It was through Kathy's network of friends, which included the Beatles, that he was able to mix with his peers. In return, as Kathy later wrote, "Jimi opened the door for me that allowed me to become myself."

Jimi and Kathy in their Mayfair flat, which was above a restaurant called Mr. Love.

chapter 3

fame's waiting room

On the evening of Saturday, October 1, exactly one week after Jimi arrived in London, the supergroup Cream were due to make their onstage debut at the **(4) Central Polytechnic** in Little Titchfield Street, off Regent Street. The concert was eagerly anticipated and the scramble for tickets among the student body had been ferocious. At the center of Cream was Eric Clapton. Born in a rural village in Surrey in 1944, the child of a wartime liaison between a teenage girl and a married Canadian Air Force officer, Clapton had been raised by his grandparents. Through art school, he had been drawn into South West London's blues scene as a teenager. By the time Jimi arrived in England, Clapton had become the country's most celebrated blues guitarist.

blues incorporated

No jazz purist despised the skiffle craze more than Alexis Korner, who wrote several hostile articles about it in the music press. Korner, born in Paris in 1928, the son of a Russian émigré and his much younger Greek wife, supported a bohemian lifestyle working as a producer for the BBC World Service, played guitar, and had been principally responsible for reviving skiffle at the 100 Club in Oxford Street. Once skiffle became a household word, he sneered at its vulgar success, perhaps a little galled that Lonnie Donegan, who had sat in on the same sessions, had taken all the credit.

Nevertheless, as young skiffle players began to explore African American music and to take their own musical skills more seriously, they naturally gravitated to Korner. In 1963 Korner opened a club in the basement of a bakery opposite the Ealing Broadway underground station. By day the space was used as a drinking club, in the evening, when the pubs opened their doors, the space was vacant. The club became the home of Korner's own blues band, Blues Incorporated. Every member of the Rolling Stones passed through Blues Incorporated at one time or another. The club was a magnet for all young musicians interested in the blues—Eric Burdon had hitchhiked all the way from Newcastle to visit it.

Coming to prominence in John Mayall's Bluesbreakers and then the Yardbirds, Clapton created the concept of the guitarist as virtuoso, a musician to be listened to, rather than danced to. Clapton made guitar playing a gladiatorial affair, and was at the pinnacle of the hierarchy of British guitar players, the undisputed champion of London. Nobody in the long line outside the Central Polytechnic jostling for admission could have guessed that Clapton's nemesis was in the building with a backstage pass.

Eric Clapton's reputation had reached New York, and Jimi had naturally been intrigued by it. Chas had held out the promise of an introduction to Clapton as an incentive for Jimi to come to London. Cream's debut was an opportunity to deliver on that promise and to launch the first phase of Chas's strategy to make Jimi a star. Jimi's work permit had come through, and Chas was eager to bring Jimi before the public. To accomplish this as quickly as possible, Chas decided to look for opportunities for Jimi to sit in with established acts, beginning with the tallest poppy.

musical differences

Apart from seeing Clapton, audience members in the know were interested to find out if Cream's bassist Jack Bruce and drummer Ginger Baker could remain onstage together without coming to blows. The two men had developed a well-known animosity when they had both worked in a jazz outfit known as the Graham Bond Organisation. Bruce, the younger of the two, had been born in 1944, in Glasgow, Scotland's second city, known for its shipyards and a culture that produces formidably abrasive men and women. As a boy, Bruce took up the cello, because the Glasgow Education Authority loaned cellos out free of charge to keep up the numbers of this unpopular instrument in the city's youth orchestras—otherwise, a musical instrument would have been beyond the Bruce family's means. Bruce proved skilful enough to win an education at the Scottish Academy of Music but gave it up to pursue a jazz career.

Baker had had no formal musical education at all. Born in 1939 in London, his father was killed in action in World War II, and he had grown up together with his sister in an impoverished single-parent household. In his teens he had discovered an affinity with the drums, and had learned his craft while he earned a living as a session player.

Notwithstanding their mutual antipathy, Bruce and Baker were of one mind as to the direction Cream should take. They wanted to follow the example of the Ornette Coleman Trio.

Ornette Coleman was born in Fort Worth, Texas, in 1930, and from his teens had played saxophone on the local R&B circuit, before traveling to Los Angeles, where he began to develop the idea of "free jazz." Coleman, and like-minded musicians such as Don Cherry, began to abandon not only structure but even melody and harmony. These ideas did not always receive a warm reception in American jazz circles, so in 1965 Coleman had moved to London, with the bassist David Izenzon and the drummer Charlie Moffet, and used the city as a base to introduce his music to Europe.

Without embracing all of Coleman's ideas, both Bruce and Baker were separately interested in forming a trio that would emphasize the musicality of all three performers through free-flowing interaction between each other, putting solo breaks before song structure. Clapton was the obvious choice for such a venture, because of his virtuosity. Baker was the first to approach him, but Clapton would agree to form the band only if Bruce was to be the bassist. So Bruce and Baker agreed to sink their differences as best they could, and accept that Clapton would work with both of them or neither of them.

The atmosphere in Cream's dressing room before the show was thick with this long-running antagonism and first-night nerves, and the arrival of Chas's forceful personality did nothing to sweeten the mood. Baker was against the idea of Jimi playing a number, which made Bruce in favor of it. Jimi meanwhile appeared to be above it all, if not out of it. He said nothing but fiddled with his exotic hairstyle and studied his reflection in the large mirror on the other side of the room.

Baker then insisted that Clapton should remain onstage for Jimi's brief appearance. When the time came, however, Clapton took the opportunity to step back and have a cigarette break. He did not take many puffs. Hendrix played the blues standard "Killing Floor," and pulled out his whole range of tricks, playing the guitar with one hand and behind his back. Clapton was the person in the theatre best qualified to see beyond the showmanship and recognize the quality of the musicianship behind it. The folklore of the American South had it that gifted bluesmen acquired their talents through communing with the spirit world at crossroads at midnight. Clapton had spent his life in pursuit of the essence of the blues; now, at his hour of triumph, it seemed as if some restless crossroads spirit from the Mississippi Delta had risen among the red double-decker buses at the busy intersection of Oxford Circus and come and claimed it back.

rags and riches

The following week the Experience began rehearsing in the offices of the Animals' music publishers, **(5) Clarins**, 17 Savile Row. This narrow, even gloomy street that runs behind Regent Street is famous for its world-class tailoring businesses. It is a place of industry rather than trade. The wealthy clientele drop in for fittings, but the life of the street is the skilled tailors who sew and stitch by hand on the premises.

It is an unlikely address from which to begin a rock band, and an unsuitable one. Even tucked away at the end of a corridor, the Experience could be heard throughout Clarins' offices. One afternoon an exasperated visitor put his head around the door and asked them to keep the noise down. They later found out he was Henry Mancini, the film composer still remembered for the *Pink Panther* theme.

On the first day of rehearsals Mitch Mitchell asserted himself. "In the Midnight Hour" had been fine as an audition piece, but when Hendrix suggested they begin with it, Mitchell refused. As far as he was concerned, he had enough of bashing out soul covers.

Mitchell's hero of the time was Elvin Jones, the drummer with the John Coltrane Quartet, and Mitchell wanted to use the sparseness of the Experience's lineup as a space in which to experiment and stretch himself as a musician. Chandler was ready to sack Mitchell on the spot for his insubordination, but Hendrix welcomed the challenge. For the time being "In the Midnight Hour" remained in the set, however, because there was as yet no original material.

Also in the repertoire was "Hey Joe," which Chandler was still determined would be the first single. The Experience began to record demo material in **(6) Regent Studios**, 4 Denmark Street, a small studio on what is known as London's Tin Pan Alley.

rainy days and sundays

During time off from rehearsals Jimi and Kathy wandered the streets of London, relatively poor but very happy. Chas had put Jimi on a salary of £25 per week, £10 more than he paid Noel and Mitch, whom he considered hired musicians. It was the first steady income Jimi had earned since he had left the U.S. Army. (As a teenager he had enlisted in the 101st Airborne to escape Seattle, and then had himself discharged to escape the Army.) Given the weak state of Chas's finances, Jimi's income was hardly secure.

Still, it was the most Jimi had ever earned, and after the hotel bills were paid, Jimi and Kathy had enough money to amuse themselves. In the first flush of a love affair, and for Jimi the constant novelty of London, they were easily entertained. Among other things, they loved playing board games such as the London version of *Monopoly, Risk,* and even *Twister.*

They played the games with Chas and his Swedish fiancée, Lotta. The two couples socialized together intensely and shared everything. Kathy and Lotta attended the Experience's rehearsals and recording sessions, and even any business meetings Chas could arrange. Noel and Mitch sometimes tagged along to meetings too. The glue of this tight social knot was Chas's fierce possessiveness of Lotta, but the consequence was that before he had so much as a record deal or a whisper of a reputation, Jimi Hendrix had an entourage, filing in and out of the offices of A&R men together and sitting around a table in the lounge of the Hyde Park Towers laughing into the small hours. For good or ill, Jimi was to operate from the center of an entourage for the rest of his career. Even as a boy Jimi had an intense and private inner life; as his fame took off, he surrounded himself with a close circle to keep the outer world at a distance.

guitar for hire

On one excursion, Jimi took Kathy along to meet Little Richard, who was in London. Jimi, who had toured briefly with Little Richard in the States, hoped he might collect a few dollars he felt he was owed. Little Richard gave the couple a hospitable welcome in his hotel suite but was adamant that he was not handing over any money. British publicists were to make much of Jimi's apprenticeship touring the American South as a guitar for hire behind the biggest names on the R&B circuit. Many of those names—such as the Isley Brothers, James Brown, and Wilson Pickett—enjoyed enormous reputations in the British Isles, and it was assumed their lead guitarists must be equally prestigious, just as Pete Townsend all but overshadowed Roger Daltry in the Who, and Hank Marvin, lead guitar to the "British Elvis," Cliff Richard, was a star in his own right.

The truth is that for most musicians, working the R&B circuit was a miserable existence. Wages were barely at subsistence level, and were severely diminished by the arbitrary fines the star of the show felt entitled to impose on the hired help. The show was strictly a vehicle for the star, and individual musicians were given a minute at most to showcase their own talents. A minute is not a lot of time to display the extent of one's musical virtuosity, and several guitarists on the circuit had developed more immediately crowd-pleasing tricks, such as playing their guitars behind their backs. Jimi had seen and learned them all, and would use them to astonish London.

Ringo Starr's house, 34 Montagu Square, where Jimi, Kathy, Chas, and Lotta lived together. John Lennon and Yoko Ono lived there briefly a few years later.

The Hyde Park Towers Hotel, now in much better shape than when Jimi lived there with Kathy.

chapter 4

the doors swing open

the show hits the road

The Jimi Hendrix Experience made its first London appearance on Tuesday, October 25, at the Scotch of St. James. Noel, who knew nothing of Jimi's impromptu performance at the club on his first night in London, was pleasantly surprised to be beginning in such a prestigious venue.

Any work at all was welcome, as far as Chas was concerned. The launch of the Experience was a hand-to-mouth operation, and he was under an immense financial strain. Wages and studio time had to be paid for; Mike Jefferies, his supposed partner in the enterprise, had made himself all but invisible; and without gigs there was no cash flow.

As yet the Experience had no act to speak of anyway, just about twenty minutes' worth of cover versions that rode on the back of Jimi's showmanship. The showmanship was exceptional enough for the time being. The week before their first London appearance, the Experience played at the bottom of the bill in a brief tour of France headlined by the French rock-and-roll singer Johnny

Hallyday. As a warm-up act, Jimi drove the crowd at L'Olympia, Paris, wild by playing his guitar one-handed.

The week after the Experience's night at the Scotch, they crossed the Channel again for a short residency at the Big Apple Club in Munich, a popular venue for U.S. servicemen. For Noel, this was a depressing return to a circuit he was trying to escape. These were also the dates that brought home to him what he had joined. During the course of auditions and rehearsals Noel had found nothing remarkable in Jimi's playing. He was thus astonished, and a little frightened, to witness Jimi drive the audience at the Big Apple to a frenzy in such a confined space. From the stage, Noel felt that the audience was no longer in possession of itself and might reach out and tear the band to pieces. Noel suddenly realized that behind Jimi's genial manner lurked something passionate and dangerous.

the fast track

Both Jimi and Chas wanted more from the Experience than a novelty act, and both realized that the time for development was limited by the need to earn. Matters symbolically came to a head on the eve of the French tour, when Chas walked into Jimi's room at the Hyde Park Towers and presented him with a blue mohair suit. Jimi knew the drain this gift was on Chas's limited resources and accepted it with all the good grace he could muster. Privately he was dismayed and insulted. He had been forced to wear such outfits when he toured behind the big names of the R&B circuit, and the sight of it reminded him of past humiliations. Fortunately, the night at the Scotch was to change everything.

In the Scotch that night were Kit Lambert and Chris Stamp, the managers of the Who. Kit was the son of the composer Constant Lambert, who had written for the ballet and who had helped introduce the jazz idiom into the classical repertoire during the 1920s. Chris was the brother of the actor Terence Stamp, a rising working-class talent, and to be authentically working class was impossibly chic, so Terence had been interviewed at length for *Time*'s "Swinging London" article. Chris and Terence were the sons of a Thames waterman, a member of an artisanal brotherhood skilled in navigating London's tricky tidal waterway, and whose family connections with the river stretched back to Shakespeare's day and beyond.

Kit and Chris had become friends while working as production assistants at Shepperton Film Studios in the southwestern suburbs of London. Their involvement with music had begun when they decided to make a documentary about a pop group. With barely any idea how to begin the project, Kit happened to see a group known as the High Numbers playing in a pub. He introduced himself, and with his camp grandeur made a dazzling impression. He was equally taken by the High Numbers' boisterous energy, and during the course of a boozy evening it was agreed that Kit would abandon his documentary, the High Numbers would abandon their manager, and Kit and Chris would manage the group. The next morning Kit went into Shepperton Studios hung-over to inform Chris of the interesting turn his career had taken in his absence.

Kit and Chris proved adroit managers, with a special flair for publicity. They renamed the High Numbers the Who; devised the finale in which the band apparently destroyed their equipment at the end of their set; and Kit in particular worked to associate the Who with the Mod movement in the minds of newspaper editors, all the better to generate scandalous headlines.

Actual Mods cared nothing for the Who and were, if anything, contemptuous of the band's claim to be associated with them. The Mod movement had caught the public imagination through newspaper reports of violence between motor scooter-riding Mods and motorcycle-riding Rockers at seaside resorts on public holidays. This ready-made notoriety was a useful publicity lever for Kit Lambert to pull.

"Mod" was a newspaper label, and the young men around which the term was shaped had no interest in violence for its own sake and a very limited interest in motor scooters. Mod was not a tribal movement at all; to the contrary, it celebrated individualism to the point of narcissism. Mods were working-class dandies.

In Britain's industrial North, working-class communities were built around attachments to large enterprises such as cotton mills, shipyards, and coal mines. Dependence on one available source of employment created a warm mutuality in working-class culture, but also a fierce conformity and a suspicion of anyone who made too much of themselves. In London, where there was much more economic variety—with unskilled workers able to find casual work with small enterprises or in the freewheeling street markets—there was a stronger tradition of self-reliance and independence of mind in working-class life.

Elements of Mod style—such as the bell-bottom trousers and the peaked cap—can be traced back to the original Hooligans, the young men who worked as barrow boys in London's street markets at the end of the nineteenth century and outraged the Victorian middle class with their insolence.

"Mod" was an abbreviation for "modernist," however, and the Mods took inspiration from the modern world, which offered them a garden of earthly delights such as no generation of working-class youth had seen before. Mods took a disdainful view not only of the Who but of mass culture in general. Socially, they danced to Motown and Stax at clubs such as the Scene in Soho. Privately, they listened to the modern jazz of Dave Brubeck, Stan Kenton, and John Coltrane. Mods looked for new ideas not only over the Atlantic but over the English Channel too. They ignored the prêt-à-porter of Carnaby Street, and ordered their own bespoke designs from the local tailors, taking their ideas from the Italian styles they had seen in Fellini movies. The more sophisticated explored existentialism through the novels of Jean-Paul Sartre and Albert Camus.

Kit and Chris were as spontaneously excited by the potential of the Experience as they had been by the High Numbers. "They all but knocked over the tables, that night in The Scotch, in their rush to get to me," Chas recalled. Once they realized that Chas was not going to allow them to prise the management of Jimi away from him, Kit had another, very welcome proposition. Kit and Chris were setting up an independent record label, Track Records, to help the Who escape the conservatism of the major labels. Would Chas be interested in a record deal?

Even before this invitation, the Experience had begun recording their first single, and moved their activities to the (7) **De Lane Lea Studios**, 129 Kingsway, where the business district of the City of London begins to melt into the shops and restaurants of London's West End. De Lane Lea shared a building on the corner of Kingsway and Great Queen Street with a bank, and there was some tension when the bank alleged that the vibrations of Experience rehearsals were disrupting its experiments with an early computing system.

Chas had been in negotiation with executives at the major label Decca, but after they heard the tape of "Hey Joe" they turned it down, just as they had turned down the Beatles four years previously. Kit Lambert pounced on the opportunity, understanding the urgent need for success of some kind. Track Records was not due to launch until March 1967, but he used his influence to persuade Polydor, who were to act as Track's distributor, to release "Hey Joe" on their own label as a one-off. Polydor was a German record company that had recently opened a London office, staffed by just one A&R man, to see if they could grab a corner in the British beat market.

Meanwhile the band's straitened circumstances and an uncertain future were breeding an esprit de corps. Noel, a bassist now, sold his guitar amp to generate extra cash. Chas sank his masculine pride and allowed Lotta to take a part-time job as a cloakroom attendant at a club, and then changed his mind when a fight broke out there on her first Saturday night. Kathy was terrified that Jimi would have to go back to New York.

With no support from Jefferies, barely any record deal to speak of, and no imminent work, Chas decided to make something happen. He sold a couple of his own bass guitars to fund a press launch.

The venue was the **(8) Bag O'Nails**, 10–11 Kingly Street, a narrow road between Carnaby Street and Regent Street barely wide enough for two cars to pass each other. The event was held at lunchtime on the last Wednesday of November, and to generate enough buzz to attract London's large music press every string was pulled to pack the basement with famous faces. The cellar club was a regular haunt of John Lennon and Paul McCartney, both of whom turned up to the launch.

The brief performance did not get off to the best of starts. Few there knew what to expect, and the sheer noise when the band played caused some people to flee the building. After a short set, the Experience retreated to their dressing room to await judgment. There was a knock at the door and John Lennon burst in, Paul McCartney close behind him. A few days short of his twenty-fourth birthday, Jimi had the much-mobbed Beatles mobbing him.

chapter 5

ready, steady, go

a frightening performance

A few days before Christmas 1966, Chris Welch, features writer at *Melody Maker*, finally caught up with latest word-of-mouth sensation on the London club circuit. As always in the run up to Christmas, central London was awash with parties, and for Welch the days had merged into a blur. The evening he first saw Hendrix he had already seen the Who play a club date in Walthamstow in North London, before driving to (9) **Blaises Club**, 121 Queen's Gate, Kensington. Like the Scotch, Blaises was a venue for insiders, "where musicians, agents, managers and writers allowed themselves to be deafened, whilst imbibing quantities of alcohol," in Welch's words. When he arrived that night, nobody was acting too cool to care, however.

> The club was packed and the only way to see Jimi was to stand on tip-toe and crane the neck. In the squashed and steaming crush around the pocket-sized stage, I glimpsed my first sighting of Jimi Hendrix, and scribbled Jimmy Hendricks in my ink stained notebook.
>
> Jimi stood crouched over his guitar, rocking back and forth in the few square feet normally reserved for

boogalooing. When he lifted his guitar to his teeth and noises screeched from the amplifier it seemed almost frightening. It was expected that blood would fleck from his lips or volts of electricity would course though his body.

It was not quite Welch's first sighting of Jimi. Chas had introduced them to each other earlier in the autumn. "The first faint recollection of meeting him was a nervous 'Hello' at a party in some long forgotten flat. Jimi sat on the floor in a corner and didn't say anything. Nobody seemed to say much to him either."

in search of secrets

Chris Welch was not the only person to be taken by surprise by the difference between Jimi's personality onstage and offstage. Pete Townshend had been underwhelmed when Jimi had introduced himself to the Who's guitarist at De Lane Lea Studios. "I was very unimpressed with Jimi that day, he was wearing a beat up US Marines Jacket, and he looked scruffy, jetlagged and pock marked. I thought 'Ugh'."

Jimi had approached Pete for advice, something he was never ashamed to seek. When on tour through the South, he had always used his time off to seek out the best guitarist in town, pursuing both the famous and the unknown without guile or flattery but with a great deal of persistence and many direct questions. There was no keeping a technical secret from Jimi; if he wanted to know something, he followed you around until he found it out.

So when Pete Townshend was pointed out to him, Jimi seized the opportunity to question him about Marshall amplifiers, because nobody knew more about them than Pete. He knew Jim Marshall, the founder of the firm rather than the inventor of the amp, personally and had been involved in the development of the prototypes through voluble but constructive criticism. "In the old days I used to storm into Jim Marshall's shop and swear at him. They'd run to build something new, and I'd come back the next day to say that it wasn't loud enough, or it wasn't good enough. In the end I got what I wanted," he recalled in an interview in 2000.

shepherds bush sound

Jimi went out of his way to make the amp-builder's acquaintance too, going with Mitch to **(10) Jim Marshall's** shop at 93 Uxbridge Road, Hanwell, on the road toward Ealing in late December. There, in an ordinary, if not even slightly dismal parade of shops, Jim Marshall kept a drum and guitar store that, together with the workingman's cafe next door, had become one of the hubs of the London music scene.

The business had started in 1960, as the retail arm of Jim Marshall's drum tuition business. Unlike other veteran musicians of the big band era, Marshall had not dismissed rock and roll as a cheap fad. A tough-minded entrepreneur from an extended family of boxers, he was happy to teach kids who wanted to learn rock-and-roll styles—provided they had the guinea an hour he charged for lessons.

Through his young pupils Marshall was plugged into the network of musicians in West London who were moving from rock, through pop, to blues. And once he started selling drum kits, it was natural to diversify into guitars and then into amps.

Mitch had been one of Marshall's pupils and protégés, and the Saturday job he had in the drum shop as a schoolboy had given him his first contacts in music. When he took Jimi out to Shepherds Bush to meet Jim Marshall that December afternoon, Jimi became just one of several guitarists who had met Jim through his drummer.

Jimi was not shy when he was introduced to Jim. He announced himself as the greatest guitarist in the world. Jim, who knew both Pete Townshend and Jeff Beck well, preferred to reserve his judgment on this. As a business man before anything else, he was wary that Jimi and Mitch had come to try and talk him into an endorsement deal. Even if Jimi Hendrix was the greatest guitarist in the world, as far as Jim was concerned he would pay cash like everyone else.

Jimi's claims may have reinforced Jim's prejudice that all Americans were arrogant, but Jimi's charm won the day. Jimi made much of the coincidence that they shared the same name, they were both James Marshalls. Jim was left with the impression of a serious-minded and knowledgeable young man. Jimi for his part was determined to work with Marshall amps as soon as he could afford them.

the marshall sound

That Jimi had never come across Marshall amps before he arrived in London was hardly surprising. They were constructed in the backroom of Jim's shop. The first proper assembly line had been set up only in June 1964, and it was a modest affair. Before that, all Marshall amps had been built by two teenage electronics enthusiasts, Kevin Bran and Dudley Craven, with valves salvaged from army surplus stores. The wooden housings for the amps and the speaker cabinets were built by Jim Marshall in his home, from which he also ran a poultry business.

PA systems in London in the 1960s were primitive and carried only the vocals. Even internationally successful beat bands such as the Beatles did not work with monitors, the small amps that relay a band's performance back to the players onstage. Mixing desks were unheard of. All the audience heard of the guitarists was what came through the guitar amp. This was usually more than the guitarist himself heard. Standing with an amp and a rowdy crowd in front of him and a full drum kit behind him, the guitarist could barely hear himself play. As often as not, the drummer could hear nothing of what the rest of the band were doing.

It was a problem Jim Marshall understood very well. As a young man, exempt from military service for health reasons, he had been a musician during the Blitz, singing as a crooner while simultaneously playing the drums. Although he had had a limited education, Marshall had taught himself electronic engineering during his day job, and had built his own PA system to carry his soft vocals over his snare drum and cymbals. Now a middle-aged business man, he was shrewd enough to make way for youth, and left the development of the amp that has made his name world famous to Kevin, originally hired as a repairman, and Dudley, who had been lured away from a job at the record label EMI for a salary of £15 a week, an extraordinary one for an eighteen-year-old.

Marshall and his team's success was built on an important technical insight. Historically, amplifiers had been built to eliminate as much surplus noise as possible. This is because amplifiers had been made chiefly to deliver the human voice. Marshall's team recognized that an amplifier valve, driven to just below the point it explodes, vibrates and adds harmonics to the notes, giving a truer reproduction of a plucked string. The pursuit of power alone produced a much richer tone.

a london home

In December Jimi and Kathy left the Hyde Park Towers Hotel to move to **(11) 34 Montagu Square** with Chas and Lotta. Kathy had negotiated the move. The property was under lease to Ringo Starr, and when Kathy ran into him one night and mentioned that she and Jimi were looking for somewhere more permanent, he offered to sublet the house to them.

The London square is a form of residential architecture that flourished between the seventeenth and nineteenth centuries. The facades of the terraced houses on all four sides of a London square face each other across communal gardens in the center. Although each side of the square is built as one continuous block, it is divided into tall private houses rather than apartments. Luxurious in their use of space, and secluded and exclusive in their architecture, the squares were built for the wealthy. The inward-looking design discourages through traffic, and the communal gardens are enclosed with iron railings and padlocked, so only residents can use them.

Ringo had fitted the place out with James Bond–style opulence, although certain period features could not help but obtrude. As Kathy recalls in her memoirs: "It consisted of the ground and lower-ground floors of a converted town house in a smart square near Marble Arch. Chas and Lotta had a white-carpeted bedroom on the ground floor, opposite the sitting room, while Jimi and I were downstairs in a room opposite the kitchen. Upstairs had an en-suite bathroom with a pink sunken bath, which seemed very exotic to us, and Jimi and I had a bathroom with doors off the kitchen, and a dressing room. Our bedroom had a horrible old fireplace at one end and a lot of paneling on the walls but it was still the best place I had ever lived and seemed a fitting home for a rising pop star."

Jimi was indeed a rising pop star, even if, according to Chas, he, Jimi, Kathy, and Lotta had no more than thirty shillings (less than £2) between them. "Hey Joe" was released in early December and became a club hit. It failed to make much radio penetration, however, either on the BBC or the "pirate stations" such as Radio Luxembourg. Radio playlists were largely based on chart success, and an initial chart entry required chicanery that lay beyond Chas's means.

There were several influential pop charts—including the BBC's, *Melody Maker's,* and Radio Luxembourg's—and all were based on extrapolations from sales in a handful of "chart return" record shops. These stores, their identity supposedly a secret, logged and reported their sales to the chart compilers, and these figures were then blown up to reflect a supposed national picture. In the careless 1960s the roster of chart return shops was seldom changed, and every self-respecting record promoter had a copy of it. Some individuals made a freelance living by going around the chart return shops buying up singles on behalf of the artist's management. Too short of money to pay for such services, Chas sent Kathy out to do this.

"Hey Joe" was boosted by a television appearance on the pop program *Ready Steady Go!* in the middle of December. In the 1960s Britain television played an especially important role in bringing what was developing in the subculture of clubs and discotheques to a wider public. Radio was pop music's natural medium, but in the early 1960s very little airtime was given over to it. The BBC had a national monopoly over radio, and until the 1970s there were no commercial radio stations in Britain. In addition to the natural conservatism of a public broadcasting company with a remit to please everybody, the BBC was limited to how much needle time it could give to pop music by a longstanding agreement with the Musicians' Union.

The BBC, which had half a dozen full orchestras on its payroll, was the largest employer of musicians in the country, if not the world. This gave the Musicians' Union a lot of leverage in its battle with the professional musician's natural enemy, the gramophone record. The union used this leverage to limit the number of hours of recorded music the BBC could broadcast, and insisted that the hits of the day be played live by the BBC's own musicians. During the big band era there was not much to distinguish between the Glen Miller Orchestra's "In The Mood" and the BBC Dance Orchestra's version. With the beat group revolution, the agreement became absurd. Melodious as Lennon and McCartney tunes can be, "I Wanna Hold Your Hand" loses something of its urgency when arranged for strings.

music in black and white

It was left to television to satisfy the national hunger for pop music. The BBC had introduced the weekly program *Top of the Pops* in 1964, which was based around artists miming to their records surrounded by an audience free to dance in a studio designed to look like a disco. *Top of the Pops'* strength and weakness was that it was based strictly around the BBC's top thirty with the emphasis on the top ten. Consequently, the Rolling Stones might appear alongside an artist such as Val Doonican, an Irishman given to performing sentimental songs from a rocking chair.

The BBC had no monopoly over television. A commercial network had been introduced in the 1950s, and independent television countered *Top of the Pops* with the more adventurous *Ready Steady Go!* The show had the same open studio format but the musicians played live to the audience (the show itself was recorded). *Ready Steady Go!* was dedicated to pop music, and its independence from the charts gave the producers freedom to showcase acts that were as yet no more than a metropolitan buzz. One of the producers, Vicki Warham, had seen Jimi and the Experience at their Scotch appearance and had been as excited as Kit Lambert and Chris Stamp.

The show drew an enormous audience—in the 1960s most television shows did, because there were only two channels to choose between. For provincial Britain, *Ready Steady Go!* and *Top of the Pops* were windows into Swinging London—and provincial Britain was not always enchanted with what it saw. As someone signing themselves "Disgusted Viewer, Newcastle on Tyne" wrote to a Sunday newspaper the following year:

> I have been watching Top Of The Pops, and believe me if I had to give a cup to the leading nitwits of the programme it would be between The Move and Jimi Hendricks Group [sic]. The first lot were absolutely stupid. I am sure the drummer must have suffered from the itch or something. As for the Hendrick's group, I hope I never meet any of them in the dark, with their hair sticking out like huge mops. Hendricks himself looks awful because of the way he dresses. Heaven preserve us from such. I know it takes all sorts to make a world, but do they ever take a long look at themselves?

chapter 6

dicky birds, dolly birds, and woof tickets

finding a voice

The riff that was to become "Purple Haze" first emerged in a dressing room in a remote corner of northeast London in mid-December. Forest Gate was and still is a crowded, noisy, and otherwise utterly unremarkable district crammed between London's East End and Epping Forest, twelve miles of wild countryside saved from development at the end of the nineteenth century that has served as a Cockney retreat ever since. In the 1960s this bleak district enjoyed a splash of glamour in the shape of the **(12) Upper Cut Club**, Earlham Grove, set up in a converted cinema (the building has now been leveled to a car park) by local boxing champion Billy Walker. The neighborhood offered little in the way of distractions for visiting musicians, so when the Experience was booked into the Upper Cut, Jimi killed the time before going onstage by playing his guitar in the dressing room. It was Chas who saw the riff's potential. "Keep that," he said.

Jimi had nurtured the dream of becoming a songwriter ever since 1965 when he had heard Bob Dylan's "Like a Rolling Stone." Hendrix's devotion to Dylan was intense—and highly unusual for a musician on the American R&B circuit of the early 1960s.

Jimi had been as baffled as anyone else from his background would be when he first encountered Dylan, and then delved further into the Minnesotan's back catalogue: the reedy voice, the strummed guitar, the elliptical lyrics—it was all a long way from James Brown. But Jimi was eclectic in his tastes—Dean Martin had been his first musical hero—and he was persistent in the face of things he did not understand. He persevered until he grasped that the point was the words and then he marveled at their power. One of the few things he brought to London with him was a Bob Dylan songbook.

In New York Jimi had begun the habit of jotting down a line here or there on a napkin and storing these ideas in his guitar case. But nothing ever materialized from these scribbled thoughts, and periodically they vanished, along with his guitar case, when he had a guitar stolen. The source of the words of "Purple Haze" was a dream inspired by a sci-fi novel.

Moving into Montagu Square gave Jimi the run of Chas's large collection of sci-fi fiction. At their first meeting at the Cafe Wha?, Chas had left Jimi with a copy of *Earth Abides* by Chuck D. Weiss. This pioneering story of eco-catastrophe, which tells of a group of people returning to the way of life of Native Americans after the collapse of industrial society, could not have been calculated better to appeal to Jimi, who felt his Native American ancestry very deeply, and he immediately became a devotee of the genre.

The idea of a purple haze came from the novella *Night of Light* by Philip Jose Farmer, which had been published that year. In *Night of Light* the purple haze is an atmospheric condition that affects a distant planet and causes those who dare to expose themselves to it to live their dreams in a fully waking state. In the purple haze, the book's hero, Joe Dante, finds himself driven by compulsions that he is able to act upon as precisely as if they sprang from his rational will, all the while watching the consequences with his normal state of mind. The consequences of Joe's actions in the purple haze are appalling because he finds himself driven to brutally murder his wife over and over again. As he does so he realizes that his compulsion springs from his desire to punish her for the neglect he suffered from his wayward mother.

why can't the english teach their children how to speak?

Another stimulus to Jimi's imagination was his engagement with British English, with its amazing variety of dialects for a small island, and the variety of accents it is spoken in. As many musicians are, Jimi was a skilful mimic, and he playfully set to work mastering the many different accents he heard around him, beginning with Chas's very distinctive Geordie accent.

Even the orthodox usage of the BBC could take Jimi by surprise and stimulate his imagination. "I heard big impressive words spoken on telly," he told his friend the American journalist Sharron Lawrence. "I'll never forget watching the news and a reporter speaking of 'uncharted waters.' Ever since I have wanted to use 'unchartered waters' in a song. That's life in a nutshell. Hearing English spoken in England was like opening a door."

London was also, as always, alive with unorthodox and unofficial slang. London slang is fast changing, much influenced by fashion, and always popular in a crowded city full of communities such as immigrants, market traders, and, of course, criminals, who wish to talk among themselves without being understood by outsiders. Anything exclusive acquires glamour and attracts curiosity, and in London, where high life and low life often rub elbows and a good deal more besides, the transition is speedy and the turnover of slang swift.

In the 1960s the slang that was moving from the street to the parlor was Polari. Polari emerged among traveling show people, fairground workers, and actors at the end of the nineteenth century. Its origins are obscure but because many words in Polari appear to have their roots in Italian (*bona* for "good," *omi* for "man"), it is assumed to have been spread by the Italian immigrants who wandered Britain as street entertainers.

By the middle of the twentieth century Polari had been adopted by gay men as a means of recognizing one another. Just as other gay signals such as pink shirts became a driving influence on mainstream men's fashion, so Polari seeped into artistic circles and through to middle-class respectability. Given the rising public sympathy at the time for the decriminalization of homosexual acts, the use of the word *palaver* for "fuss," say, had a liberal tinge. The general climate of liberalization also required words for ideas that had not been expressed openly before, and Polari was able to supply them. *Drag,* the Polari word for any glamorous outfit, came to be used for cross-dressing. And Polari supplied the two words that encapsulated the era, "dolly birds" (*dolly* is Polari for "pretty" and *bird* means "woman").

selling woof tickets

Noel contributed a cultural element that opened new possibilities for Jimi to express himself: English nonsense humor. In January 1967, when the Experience returned to London from provincial gigs in the early hours, Jimi would go to Noel's room in the Madison Hotel to smoke Moroccan hashish and listen to records, especially Noel's favorite comedy records by the Goons. Spike Milligan, the principal writer and performer of the 1950's BBC radio program *The Goon Show,* joined Jimi's pantheon of great writers.

Spike was born Terence Allen Milligan in Ahmednarg in India in April 1918, a child of the British Empire and the son of an

Irish-born army sergeant. In 1939, when war broke out with Germany, Spike was called up into the Royal Artillery. The army was to be the central experience of his life. It gave him the stability to catch up on his education through private reading, allowed him to form his own jazz band, and let his personality flourish in the role of company jester. Unfortunately, it also sent him into battle. Spike fought in Egypt and Italy until he was wounded at the battle of Monte Cassino. The wound may or may not have been the cause of the bipolar syndrome that tormented him for the rest of his life.

Beneath the nonsense of the Goons lay a bleaker strata from Spike's depressive bouts, the perspective of the enlisted man for whom the world is a dangerous place run by unprincipled nincompoops. The show, said Spike, "represents the permanency of man, his ability to get through anything and survive, albeit through stupidity."

Jimi had a gift for comedy himself. One of his favorite devices was the shaggy dog story, a tale that begins plausibly enough but that gradually grows more and more fantastic. Jimi would deliver his shaggy dog stories in a composed and matter-of-fact fashion until, just as his listeners began to doubt, he would shout "Woof, Woof!" as a signal that they had been had. He called this game "selling a woof ticket."

Jimi displays his playful side at a record launch in December 1967.

chapter 7

hearing secret harmonies

the lion and the lamb

In the middle of January Jimi and the Experience returned to the Bag O'Nails. It was not two months since they had held their press launch there. This Wednesday evening the club was filled not by hype but word of mouth. The audience was made up of musicians, not critics, here to see if everything they had heard was true.

The music journalist Penny Valentine recorded the evening in her diary:

> Hendrix appears at The Bag O'Nails in Kingly Street. We go along. Pete Townshend is there and Eric Clapton is almost unrecognizable. Just back from Paris, he looks like a slender French mod with a cropped haircut and tight-fitting pastel cashmere sweater. By the time Hendrix comes on stage, this club is so hot and full that condensation is running down the walls. Sweat is running down my back as Hendrix starts the stamping, heaving introduction to "Purple Haze". "I can't see him," I wail. I am beginning to feel faint in the crush and wish that I had not had three virulently coloured tequila sunrises. Someone lifts me up

onto their shoulders so I can see the stage. Young, skinny, black with a halo of curls, Hendrix holds his guitar slung low and slightly away from his body but makes it roar defiantly, even though it doesn't look like his fingers are moving. He finishes by getting on his knees, and playing with his teeth. We are stunned. I have a momentary panic that Hendrix will electrocute himself. Pete and Eric have their mouths open but say nothing and Hendrix finishes with a flourish of feedback and wailing anger. When he comes offstage to talk to Townshend and Clapton he is so shy and deferential we all feel bewildered.

The same week saw "Hey Joe" make the top thirty, a month after its release. The industry buzz surrounding Jimi had woken Mike Jeffries' interest in his partnership with Chas. One of his first actions was to take the record plugging out of Kathy's hands and to put some serious investment behind the single. This included buying airtime on the offshore pirate radio stations. The BBC was resolutely and incorruptibly uncommercial. The pirate stations, which broadcast constant pop music from ships off the British coast, happily swapped airtime for cash.

enter the boffin

Among those eager to introduce themselves to Jimi at the Bag O'Nails was a young man named Roger Mayer. A maker and inventor of electronic sound effects, he was only a few days past his twenty-first birthday but had already heard sounds he had created on number one records.

The son of an electrical engineer, he had been born in Sutton, Surrey, a small town on the edge of Southwest London. In 1967 he was a civilian employee of the Royal Navy, based at the Admiralty Research Laboratories in Teddington, a Southwest London suburb beside the River Thames, where he was conducting research into submarine warfare.

Roger had begun experimenting with guitar effects as a school-boy and built his first fuzz box at the age of fifteen. He made it for his school friends, Jimmy Page and Jeff Beck. Roger's guitar laboratory was very much a bedroom operation, with the welding done at his father's factory. Jimmy Page repaid the favor by introducing Roger to his blues collection. It was a typical teenage friendship, with Jimmy, Jeff, and Roger dropping in on each other's houses after school to play records and experiment with guitars. As Jimmy and Jeff began to perform in public, Roger met other musicians on Southwest London's remarkable teen music scene, such as Eric Clapton, who attended a neighboring school, and the boys who were forming themselves into what would become the Rolling Stones, farther up the river in Richmond on Thames. Roger's sister was a student at St. Martin's College of Art in the West End of London, and he introduced him to the soul records that were played in fashionable clubs such as the Scene in Soho's Ham Yard. Together they went to the first Rolling Stones' gigs on Eel Pie Island, in the Thames at Twickenham.

box of tricks

A short, vivacious man with an outgoing personality, Roger had nothing of the geek about him and plunged into conversation with Jimi. They had much to talk about, in particular Roger's latest invention, the Octavia pedal.

The basic function of an Octavia is to play a note from an electric guitar one octave higher than it would naturally sound. This simple idea requires complex execution. In the natural world of acoustic instruments it is easy to add a lower octave to a guitar: you just lengthen the neck. This is why bass guitars are taller than ordinary guitars. Producing a higher octave is another matter. On a bass guitar the first octave is about the length of a man's shoulder to his wrist. The second is about the width of his out stretched hand. The third, hypothetical higher octave would be about the span of two fingers. It is like folding a piece of paper in half eight times: easy to conceive, but physically impossible to accomplish.

Jimi invited Roger to bring the device along to a gig, and it was agreed that they would meet up when the Experience played in the **(13) Chislehurst Caves**, Caveside Close, Chislehurst, Kent, ten days later. There, in an extraordinary venue set in a network of tunnels, some of which date back to the Stone Age, Jimi tried out the Octavia and was enthusiastic. They next met a few days later at the **(14) Ricky Tick Club**, 1-1A, High Street, Hounslow, a low-ceilinged space above a shop in a boxlike, red brick arcade of shops in Hounslow, a district of London that had grown up after World War II to fill in the space between London and Heathrow Airport. Jimi had studio time booked for after the gig, but proceedings were delayed when he put his Stratocaster through the Ricky Tick's ceiling and bent a couple of machine heads out of shape. Noel went out into the night to borrow a Telecaster, and it was this, together with Roger's Octavia, that was used to overdub two solos in the small hours: "Purple Haze" and "Fire." As Roger recently recalled: "That was the beginning. In the four or five weeks since I'd met him we'd produced the definitive second record of his."

It was a beginning. From then on Roger was a fixture at every recording session and went to as many Experience gigs as he was able to, between eighty or ninety in his estimation, as well as being present at countless after-hours jams.

Roger also became a frequent visitor to Montagu Square, sitting in on the games of *Risk* that were often set up for days on end, and becoming one of the few visitors to ever catch a glimpse of Jimi in his hair rollers, a sight kept well guarded from the public view and that Jimi was embarrassed about even among close friends.

Another enthusiasm Roger shared with Jimi was science fiction. All the young scientists at the Admiralty read science fiction as a form of mental relaxation when a scientific problem appeared to have reached a dead end. In Roger, Jimi found a friend with boundless energy for experimentation and a perfectionist by nature, and also someone with whom he could articulate his ideas about what music was and what it could accomplish.

Their friendship gave further cause for concern to London's established guitarists, already taken aback by the Bag O'Nails performance. Jimi was a formidable threat to their reputations on his own; with Roger by his side, Jimi would dazzle as never before.

The onstage Jimi who frightened Penny Valentine was just as competitive as his rivals. The offstage Jimi took a more casual attitude that could be far more embarrassing to a guitarist who cherished his reputation. "He was so open to play with anybody, musically he scared a lot of people who didn't want to play with him," Roger remembers.

> A lot of people were put off but if you were round there and he was playing he'd hand you a guitar. "Come on Roger, let's jam. Oh it's upside down, don't worry about that!" He was very keen for people to participate and have fun and play with him. He didn't care, he'd go to a club, he'd play the bass, he'd play the guitar upside down, this way round, just have a bit of fun, you know. He was always up for it. Not like some people, and we won't mention names, but some people who play the guitar and are very well known, it doesn't come easy for them and consequently if they haven't practiced their little solo, if they're not in their own environment, they're not going to get up and jam. They're not going to show you how good they're not. And Jimi, like, blew those guys apart. It was like: "Christ is he really that good?" "You want to know? Yes he is that good. Any day of week, any time of the day, in any condition, he's one hot guitar player."

taking off

A stimulus to Jimi's imagination was the discovery of Gustav Holst's *Planet Suite.* The move to Montagu Square gave Jimi access to a record player, in the form of a large stereo radiogram, and, with income coming in from gigs, he began to build a record collection. The *Planet Suite* was an impulse buy—Jimi was simply attracted to the cover—but the work soon appealed to deeper sympathies. Holst, a prolific composer, had been music master at St. Paul's Girls School in Hammersmith from 1905 until he retired in the 1920s, and had lived a short walk from where Jimi was now recording. The *Planet Suite,* a musical portrait of the solar system, had been inspired by astrological lore. Jimi was also intrigued by the idea of the musical voyage, of a journey on which music could take the listener into new spaces and different places. "We were interested, Jimi and I, in taking someone on a space journey, it would take them out, the sound of the guitars," Roger recalled. Just like NASA, Jimi and Roger had their sights set on outer space, but they thought they could accomplish a moonshot with a Stratocaster rather than a Saturn V.

chapter 8

magic fingers

on the road again

During the first two months of 1967 Jimi, Noel, and Mitch worked hard together in the highest of spirits. Success made little material difference to their lives; it just meant more time spent in the van on the road, a lifestyle with which all three young men were already familiar. In January they played twenty dates and in February twenty-four, criss-crossing England to perform wherever booking agencies sent them.

Sometimes they found themselves on the working-man's club circuit, social clubs founded around industrial trades, where the band shared the bill with comedians and perhaps a stripper, and the audience wore their hair cropped short and dressed in a collar and tie for a night out. The arrival of these ambassadors from Swinging London in colored shirts, bell-bottom trousers, and a tangle of curls piled high on their heads was greeted with suspicion. The ambassadors themselves, several hundred miles from home and with no confidence that the local police would take their side should they be called to break up a fight, encountered an air of sullen intimidation when they arrived, and they contrived to depart just as soon as they could. One night in the Northeast of England they loaded the van particularly speedily as a menacing group of onlookers gathered in the parking lot. The largest member of them approached Jimi. "Oi Nigger Boy," he shouted, "you've got magic fingers."

Jimi enjoyed telling this story to his friend Sharon Lawrence, because he knew that her liberal Californian sensibilities would cause her to wince at the use of the N word. Compared with his experiences of traveling through a Deep South that was desegregated in theory but not in practice, traveling in provincial Britain was much easier. He was sometimes perplexed at the more casual racism that ran through, and still runs through, English culture. He was shocked to discover a pub and hotel in Kathy's native Derbyshire that was named "The Black Boy."

In the first days of February Jimi took delivery of his first 200 watt stack from Jim Marshall. This added further pressure to life on the road because the valves could barely stand the power of the output and frequently blew. Even if the musicians could stay overnight in a hotel between far-flung gigs, the blown amp had to be driven back to London, repaired, and brought back. The Experience now had a roadie to handle van and equipment, Gerry Stickells, a friend of Noel's from Hastings.

one night stands

Touring had its highs as well as its lows. An appearance Jimi made at Newbury, a country town in the rural county of Berkshire, in mid-February was very lighthearted. Jimi, Noel, and Mitch killed time back stage with a water-pistol fight, together with the brother of Gerry Stickells' girlfriend. Afterwards everybody had dinner in a fish and chip shop, where Jimi signed autographs for a gaggle of fans who had gathered outside. And, of course, there were always the local girls, happy to get a brief private audience in Jimi's dressing room.

Sexual magnetism over young women is part of the mystique of the electric guitar, and Jimi, the most exceptional of electric guitarists, exerted a very exceptional magnetism indeed. The menace of his performances and his playful charm backstage were compelling and inviting. Jimi took to the sexual opportunities of touring like a Scout troop given the run of a gun shop for the afternoon. Kathy was not happy with this, and began to lose her enthusiasm for traveling with Jimi to gigs when she caught him with a woman in the cubicle of a ladies room in a Manchester club. Jimi had the grace to try to keep this side of his life away from Kathy, but he also exerted a fierce double standard over her. Although she was not inclined to be unfaithful, she was not allowed to provoke even the suspicion of jealousy.

art of noise

Busy as the Experience were, their sets were short, forty-five minutes at most. When they played within easy reach of London or at a London club, they went straight from the set to the recording studio, which was now (**15**) **Olympic Studios**, at 117 Church Street, Barnes.

Church Road, Barnes, is unlikely setting for a landmark of rock-and-roll history. A ten-minute drive south of the River Thames from the busy Hammersmith Broadway, Church Road is one of those London streets that look like they belong in a rural village. It is a winding lane of Victorian shops, with a church with eleventh-century brickwork and a fifteenth-century tower in the middle of it, set back from the road in a small churchyard with a traditional lychgate (as gateway covered with a roof). It ends with a small village green, complete with a duck pond.

Olympic Studios is at the other end of the road from the duck pond, in a building with a red brick facade that bears the date of its construction, 1906, displayed on a tablet. Sixty years later the building housed an experimental recording laboratory that produced sounds that transfixed the world. Jimi and the Experience's switch to Olympic was partly dictated by the size of its studios. Olympic's Studio A was vast enough to accommodate Jimi's sound.

The other attraction was the expertise of the engineers at the studio, which was drawing in bands such as the Small Faces and the Kinks. Even George Martin, the Beatles' producer, was known to stop by for advice.

By the standards of today, when musicians will spend months and sometimes years at work on an album, recording in the 1960s was a hasty business. The recording of *Are You Experienced?* was hastier still because Chas had a limited budget. The album was recorded and mixed within seventy-two hours of studio time.

That it was accomplished so swiftly was due to Jimi's virtuosity in the studio. The apparent recklessness of his stage performances belied his skills as a musician. "Jimi probably played the guitar more than anyone else I've ever met," recalls Roger Mayer. "Jimi used to play for hours and hours and hours—not practicing but just talking to you, and fooling round and having fun. That's what he loved to do." Jimi also had an excellent memory for music and could always repeat whatever he had played, note for note, or play it backwards if requested. He was extremely skilled at "dropping in"—that is, overdubbing a patch of a few notes onto a track he had already recorded, turning a good solo into a perfect solo.

For all his skills, Jimi was indecisive in the studio. He already had some studio experience from New York, and was a quick learner when it came to absorbing technological skills. What he lacked was both the confidence and the personality to assert himself. Jimi's London recordings are an ensemble work, rather than bearing the stamp of one dominating personality. Jimi looked to Chas for final approval of the mixes, and relied on Roger to act as his go-between in negotiations between the studio, where the musicians play, and the control room, where the sound technicians record. "I was the one who went into the studio and played with him, and went back into the control room to listen, and backwards and forwards to talk to Jimi and reassure him and be sure what we were getting in the control room was correct," Roger recalls.

Because what we were trying to do is make a bloody record. There's two different scenarios: one's playing live and the other's making a record. And they're completely different and you have to understand that. It's a big difference making a sound that's going to be played in someone's living room or car or whatever, that has to be universally acceptable for many, many different environments, a very different set of parameters than if you were playing live.

The move to Olympic Studios introduced the team to engineer Eddie Kramer, who has made the mastering and remastering of Jimi's studio performances his life's work. Born in South Africa and trained as a classical musician, Kramer became as much producer (making a creative contribution to recording) as engineer (operating the mixing desk to get the sound right). He also took charge of studio discipline. Eddie would take it on himself to tell the hangers-on to shut up or get out when things got out of hand. Jimi hated to hurt anyone's feelings.

What sapped Jimi's confidence in the studio more than anything was the attention recording drew to his singing. Jimi never, ever became reconciled to his voice; it was a source of constant frustration to him. If he could have had his way he would not have sung at all, except that he was the Experience and it was inconceivable that a front man would not sing. The perfectionist in him could hear the shortcomings of his voice and knew there was nothing he could do to bring it up to the ideal he set for himself. He felt this most acutely in the recording studio, where he had to put his guitar aside to record the vocal tracks and lay his voice bare before whoever was standing around at the time. Eddie's solution was to build a small cubicle of sound screens in the studio in which Jimi could stand to sing and pretend to himself that he was alone.

trouble and strife

After a passionate honeymoon period at the Hyde Park Towers, Jimi and Kathy, like most young couples, found cohabitation a period of disagreements and makings up. When he lost his temper, Jimi was capable of pushing and hitting Kathy. Kathy, physically defenseless as she might be, was equally violent when in a fury and threatened to take her rage out on Jimi's guitars with her high heels.

A further source of tension was Chas's attitude to Kathy. He was not happy with Jimi being in a relationship of any kind. The conventions of show-business journalism insisted that pop stars were eligible young bachelors. Managers assumed that female fans would lose interest in any pop star who was known to be spoken for.

Chas was not very happy with Kathy herself. If Jimi had to be in a relationship, Chas would have preferred it to be with somebody more biddable. The sounds of discord that rose from the basement of Montagu Square perplexed him. His own relationship with Lotta followed the traditional working-class paternalism of the Northeast of England: the man was the head of the household, and the woman knew her place. Dismayed by what appeared to him to be an unhappy relationship, Chas would take Kathy aside and suggest she should move out. Kathy stood her ground.

A frequent cause of quarrels was Kathy's cooking. Jimi was uncomfortable with the British diet, in any case—as were most visitors to London during the 1960s—and with good cause. The food was appalling.

English cuisine has never enjoyed a high international reputation, and during the 1960s the tastes acquired during wartime rationing, begun in 1939 and not fully lifted until 1954, still cast a long shadow over both domestic and restaurant kitchens. Habits of thrift still caused even first-class restaurants to serve dishes based around offal. Pigs' trotters and wild rabbits were sold in the butchers' shops. Fruit and sugar shortages had left the British people with an exceptionally sweet tooth, and they found fruit tinned in syrup an exquisite delicacy. The young and university-educated attempted to break free from this past by experimenting with French provincial cookery, inspired by popular recipe books by authors such as Elizabeth David. Experiments were limited, however, by the difficulty of obtaining the ingredients—olive oil, for instance, was only available in pharmacies, sold as a cure for earache.

Kathy had no inclination to explore French or any other cuisine. An itinerant youth, some of it spent in institutions, had left her with limited domestic skills, and she was not interested in acquiring more. One night in early spring Jimi's criticism of her cooking caused Kathy to hurl his plate to the floor and run out of the house to her friend Angie's flat to calm down. Jimi, alone in the basement lit with eerie orange flashes from a traffic signal outside, put his feelings for her into words. On her return the following morning Kathy was presented with the lyrics for "The Wind Cries Mary," her middle name. "I was not appeased" Kathy recalls. It almost diminishes the power of the song, once one knows that "the broken pieces of yesterday's life" are in fact a smashed plate and some lumpy mashed potato.

the speakeasy

For relaxation Jimi frequented the **(16) Speakeasy club**, 48 Margaret Street, which opened in January 1967 on one of the upper floors of an anonymous office building off Regent Street. The Speakeasy was an intimate, hippified space, darkly lit, low ceilinged, and furnished with old church pews and other antique furniture.

The discreet atmosphere made it attractive to stars. The Beatles were regulars. A permanent fixture at the club was a star-struck teenager called Freddie Bulsari, who was to become Freddie Mercury in the 1970s. Jimi loved the Speakeasy as a place where he could jam for as long as he wanted on the small stage while Kathy gossiped with friends. It became their second home.

The ceiling of the Ricky Tick Club on the second floor of this modest building on Hounslow High Street was so low that Jimi put his guitar through it. Nine months later he headlined at the mighty Royal Albert Hall.

chapter 9

wild thing

firestorm

Jimi crossed the threshold from musician's musician to public sensation at the end of March at the **(17) Astoria Theatre**, 232 Seven Sisters Road, Finsbury Park. The theatre was also a cinema, a 1930s' "Picture Palace," one of the grand movie theatres built in the first half of the twentieth century, set among streets of low, Victorian terrace houses that had grown up around the railway as homes for clerks and other lowly employees of the banks and stockbrokers of the mighty City of London.

The occasion was the launch of what was announced as the Walker Brothers farewell tour, before the trio of Californian musicians went their separate ways. The bill was eclectic: between the Experience at the bottom and the Walker Brothers at the top were the tuneful singer-songwriter Cat Stevens and the torch singer Engelbert Humperdinck.

It is almost needless to say that this was not the torch singer's real name. He had been born Arnold George Dorsey in Madras, India, a child of the Raj, in 1936. When he was taken on by Gordon Mills, who managed Tom Jones, another torch singer, Mills renamed Dorsey Engelbert Humperdinck after the Austrian operatic composer, on the sound grounds that once heard it was impossible to forget, and found a record deal with Decca. Overnight both Engelbert Humperdincks became household names; there was even new public interest in the original Humperdinck's opera *Hansel and Gretel.*

The opportunity to make a mark on such a tour was not to be missed. There was much discussion of what would make a good stunt. Keith Altham, a journalist from the *New Musical Express,* came up with the suggestion that Jimi set his guitar alight during "Fire." This proved easier said than done, however. A can of lighter fuel was sent for, and Chas sprayed it onto Jimi's guitar before he went on stage. When the moment came, the unrehearsed stunt was more trouble to accomplish than had been anticipated. Jimi spent several minutes on his back, striking matches before the fuel would ignite.

Then things went more dramatically than expected. From the auditorium the climax appeared to be more of a catastrophe than a stunt. "Hendrix was lying on his back playing the guitar with his teeth, when it suddenly burst into flames," Chris Welch reported in *Melody Maker* the following week. "Jimi leapt backwards and ran off stage, followed by his group. The guitar was left burning dangerously near the closed curtain and compere Nick Jones ran and tried to pick it up, burning his hands in the act. An attendant rushed on stage with a fire extinguisher and put out the flames which were rising ten feet in the air."

bad boys

Backstage tempers ignited much more swiftly than Jimi's guitar had done. The theatre manager attempted to impound Jimi's guitar as evidence. From then on Jimi and the Experience were the official bad boys of the tour, and Chas suspected that their sets were deliberately sabotaged. Stage lights malfunctioned and house lights came up with a greater frequency than one might have expected during Jimi's sets. Jimi's guitar would be found to have a broken string or be badly out of tune just before he was due on stage.

John Walker made a point of visiting the Experience dressing room to warn them against stealing the show. "Don't you dare upstage us, who do you think you are?"

Relationships were not made smoother by Noel and Mitch's mutual love of practical jokes. They stocked up with stink bombs and smoke bombs from joke shops en route, and one evening Mitch set a small clockwork robot to whirr, waddle, and spark across the stage during Engelbert Humperdinck's act.

landlord trouble

By now Jimi, Chas, Lotta, and Kathy had moved to a flat in a modern building overlooking Hyde Park across the busy Edgware Road. To Ringo Starr's embarrassment, the household had worn out their welcome among their staid neighbors in Montagu Square. One of the major influences on the choice of the new address was that it was near enough for the four of them to carry their belongings without having to hire a van—a short walk away, along a terrace of narrow early nineteenth-century houses to where the apartment building was located at the end, at **(18) 43 Upper Berkeley Street**.

There was not a great deal to be carried, just clothes, guitars, and records, and the move was accomplished in a few return trips. When he visited the flat in early April, Chris Welch noted that in spite of the splendid location, the flat itself was very sparsely furnished. The television was thick with dust from lack of use, but there was a gleaming hi-fi system.

The hi-fi system was a bit of a sore point. Noel, who had been asked to help install it, noted in his diary that it had cost £330. Even if there had been no budget for moving house, money had been found for the hi-fi. Noel and Mitch were sharing a cramped flat in Bayswater. A hierarchy was emerging, and as it emerged, it became open to question. "Once again, it was taken for granted that Chas and Lotta would have the best room and Jimi and I would get what was left," Kathy recalls in her memoirs. "Managers were often thought of being the more senior in pop partnerships in those days."

the sound and the fury

Of more concern to Noel and Mitch was that they often arrived at theatres to find promoters had billed the act as "Jimi Hendrix" with no mention of "The Experience" at all. The rising success of the Experience gave them leverage to renegotiate their pay, but they were aware they were being sidelined. Noel was under instructions from Chas to do no more on stage than sway in time.

The last person to believe the illusion that the Experience was a band rather than a star vehicle was Jimi himself. Asked by a journalist if his was a New York sound, he asserted it was pure London and had evolved with Mitch and Noel. Yet, as he recognized that he carried the show, he began to assert his authority on stage. Off stage he remained as sweet natured as ever, with a kind word for everyone and everything, including Engelbert Humperdinck's set. His onstage persona was becoming beset with frustrations that could turn the fury of his performance into rage against anything that interrupted it. As well as dealing with backstage sabotage, he had to contend with unreliable equipment, which even when it worked was not always powerful enough to overcome the roar of the crowd. A Jimi Hendrix performance was often mixture of wonder followed by disappointment as it was interrupted by technical difficulties, the disappointment felt all the more because everyone present had seen what Jimi was capable of. And nobody was more conscious of what he was capable of than Jimi. At these moments of frustration, the only physical presences he could direct his rage at or assert any control over were Mitch and Noel. When he felt Mitch was going over the top, he would bang the rim of the drum kit with his guitar.

Ambivalent as Jimi felt about being anything other than a guitarist, he was a gift to publicists. "He wasn't someone who was comfortable strutting around like a peacock," Kathy recalls. He wanted to be much cooler, although his clothes made him seem flamboyant and his highly charged sexuality was obvious to anyone who met him. "Right from the beginning he had a style of his own, wearing satin shirts with voluminous sleeves, army jackets, and bell bottoms with scarves tied around the legs long before anyone else. Even Brian Jones was still wearing suits when Jimi first arrived in London. Jimi was original in his style."

Original as it was, Jimi's taste was in synchronicity with a dramatic shift in style in London that was to go the whole world round. London's fashion houses had created the great female fashion statement of the 1960s, the miniskirt. But London's originality as a fashion center lay in the attention it gave to men's fashions, which had been stifled by convention for a hundred years.

Carnaby Street had grown up around male boutiques, catering to men who wanted to add a more exquisite touch to conventional male attire. In 1967 this dandyism exploded into Technicolor peacockery that melted the divisions between male and female fashions, and it centered on the designers who sold through the boutique Granny Takes a Trip.

granny takes a trip

(19) Granny Takes a Trip had opened at the very end of 1966 at the wrong end of King's Road in Chelsea, at number 488 opposite **(20) World's End pub**, and at the very unfashionable end of the street. To open a boutique there was the equivalent of raising a pirate flag.

Granny Takes a Trip was founded by John Pearse, who had completed a formal apprenticeship as a tailor in Savile Row, and Nigel Waymouth, a graduate of Winchester College of Art. The shop was an experience as much as a retail space, an anti-boutique in which the merchandise was carelessly displayed in an environment too dark to see it properly in any case. The shop assistants were at best offhand and at worst rude. In many ways the enterprise had more in common with punk rock than the Summer of Love (the cradle of punk rock, Malcolm McClaren and Vivienne Westwood's SEX boutique, was established at World's End, nearly a decade later). But it also encouraged the imagination and allowed young designers such as Ossie Clarke and Celia Birtwhistle a freedom to experiment that no other outlet would have given them.

Jimi had a very sensuous relationship to cloth. He traveled with a bag of ladies' silk scarves, warm to the touch and still bearing the scent of the donor. When he arrived in a hotel room, he would draw the curtains and drape scarves over the lamps until he felt at home. Noel and Mitch nick named him "the Bat" for his love of living in twilight.

the theatre glowed

For three days the Walker Brothers' tour was joined by June Southworth, a journalist for the teenybopper magazine *Fabulous 208*, which during the first half of 1967 dedicated almost its entire editorial content to the Monkees, a synthetic pop group brought together for a television sitcom that aped the madcap style of the Beatles' first two movies. The first notice *Fabulous* took of Jimi was in its April 1 issue, which, by coincidence, came out the day before the conflagration at Finsbury Park.

Fabulous, which devoted much space to pinups, ran a full-page portrait of Jimi stretched out on a sofa in a fairly conservative green suit. This was accompanied with a short paean of praise written by Steve Marriott, the lead singer of the Mod group the Small Faces. While *Fabulous* regularly ran ghost-written pieces from individual Monkees, it was unusual for a pop star to write anything for the magazine himself. For a pop star to demand editorial space to promote someone else's career was unprecedented.

Southworth was charmed by Jimi. "He was so wild on stage," she recalls, "but offstage he was gentle, quiet, warm, articulate, sensuous, and funny. Everyone who met him loved him. He was just so likeable." She was fascinated too, and in her published account of the tour (which did not appear until late June) described him lost in thought on the tour bus. "On the journey, Jimi thoughtfully chewed matchsticks and fiddled with a red rubber rose from which a Can Can dancer's shapely leg spasmodically kicked. But mostly, he looked through the window and let ideas run through his mind. These are the precious moments when an artist has time to think."

"He was an immediate sensation here," she remembers. "The image grabbed attention, but the musicianship lifted him way above his contemporaries and ensured he was here to stay. When musicians were jamming together you might get Clapton, Beck, and Page combining to produce something like the Hendrix sound, but not one of them could do it on his own. His back-to-front fingering was unique and the power was phenomenal. Theatres seemed to glow and shake when he played."

Outrageous window dressing at Granny Takes a Trip. The street environment officers of the Royal Borough of Kensington and Chelsea were not happy about this display.

chapter 10

strange brew

the keys of paradise

Lysergic acid diethylamide, LSD or "acid" for short, was a cultural rather than a chemical phenomenon. It emerged from the Swiss laboratories of Roche in the 1950s into a world that believed that it was about to unravel the secrets of the self, and that inner space would surely be colonized and conquered along with outer space.

What that conquest would result in depended on what school of psychology one was enrolled in: Behaviorists imagined a world without crime achieved through the conquest of free will, Freudians a world of pleasure through the conquest of guilt. LSD appealed to those in search of the keys to Paradise, to those who wanted the human race to retake the Garden of Eden on its own terms.

LSD is usually described inaccurately as a hallucinogen. Although hallucinations are not unusual in LSD experiences, they are not universal. There are profound visual experiences, the sense of pattern and color are vividly enhanced. Whether he or she sees demons or spends an hour studying the carpet, the LSD user feels the experience is not drawing them to another, illusory world but deeper into the nature of reality.

LSD is not a hedonistic experience—many of its effects are emotionally bruising—but for many people it was a revelation to be evangelized as widely as possible. LSD makes its subjects highly suggestible, and during the 1960s the LSD experience was highly colored by the expectations of the user.

tomorrow the world

LSD crept into London in 1965, brought in by an Englishman, Michael Hollingshead, who was a disciple of Timothy Leary, the Harvard psychology professor whose academic experiments into the psychedelic experience had mushroomed into a campaign to overthrow all knowledge that was not psychedelically inspired.

Hollingshead began his operations under the grand title of the World Psychedelic Centre. His evangelism was directed to those in high society. The headquarters of the **(21) World Psychedelic Centre** were a flat at 25 Pont Street, Belgravia, the grand residential district of eighteenth-century houses where many English aristocrats have their London address.

The LSD sessions Hollingshead hosted were highly ritualized and very different from the parties the Oregon author Ken Kesey was organizing simultaneously in San Francisco. They were held in a room dedicated to the purpose, on the night of a full moon. What was to be found in the room was strictly prescribed: hand-woven cloth, uncarved wood, flowers, ancient music, burning fire, a touch of earth, a splash of water, fruit, good bread, cheese, fermenting wine, candlelight, temple incense, a warm hand, fish swimming, and anything over five hundred years old.

The ancient music came over a sound system and light shows were projected on screens. A LSD trip at the World Centre was a guided experience, punctuated with readings from Timothy Leary's adaptation of the Tibetan Book of the Dead, to announce to the experimenters that they had crossed a *bardo,* the measures the Book of the Dead uses to divides the different levels of psychic experience, like so many floors in an elevator ride.

Another object to be find in the ritual room of the World Centre, and elsewhere on the premises, was hashish. LSD was not illegal in England in 1965 but hashish was, and a police raid closed the World Centre down six months after it opened.

a map of the underground

The three thousand hits of LSD Hollingshead had imported had already begun to leak out into less formal surroundings by then. Into the Troubadour coffee bar in the nearby Old Brompton Road, for example, and also just around the corner into a flat at **(22) Lennox Gardens**, where a brilliant young dilettante named John Dunbar lived with his beautiful young wife, Marianne Faithfull.

They were a golden couple, living off Dunbar's occasional freelance journalism and the proceeds from Faithfull's success as a pop star, a career her husband had absentmindedly launched her on. The son of diplomat, Dunbar had been born in Beirut and spent part of his childhood in Stalin's Moscow. His wide cultural horizon and gift for friendship made him the nucleus of otherwise unlikely social connections.

The couple had honeymooned in Paris with the Beat poet Allen Ginsberg and his lover Peter Orlovsky. Ginsberg had headlined at the International Poetry Festival, an audacious event organized by two graduates from Oxford University, Michael Horovitz and David Sladen. Held in the domed **(23) Royal Albert Hall**, on Kensington Gore, a large auditorium built for orchestral concerts, the event attracted an audience of seven thousand, an astonishing crowd for a poetry recital. Dunbar had been impressed at the underlying potential for a London counterculture.

Among Dunbar's wide circle of friends and acquaintances, which included the Queen's younger sister, Princess Margaret, was Peter Asher, the brother of Paul McCartney's girlfriend Jane Asher. Through this connection the Beatles were initiated into the LSD experience in the harum-scarum atmosphere of Lennox Gardens, where nobody waited for the full moon, and even the pregnant Marianne Faithfull took a trip.

The **(24) Indica Gallery**, 6 Mason's Yard, was the place where John Dunbar's eclectic interests—international art, alternative literature, and social networking—came together. Indica was built, indirectly, on Beatle money. Peter Asher had taken part in what turned out to a lucrative experiment. Uneasy as to how much of the Beatles' success was due to hype, McCartney had experimented by releasing a Lennon and McCartney song anonymously through two unknown artists. "World Without Love" by Peter and Gordon proved to be a substantial hit. As the Peter of Peter and Gordon, Asher had a lot of money that he used to found Indica, with Dunbar and the writer Barry Miles given joint ownership.

Indica was by no means a dilettante enterprise. The gallery's first show, an exhibition of Latin American artists based in Paris, sold out within days. Dunbar had entrepreneurial acumen as well as social panache. Above all, he had an adventurous disposition and nurtured what is now known as conceptual art. In the spring of 1967 Indica hosted a show by Yoko Ono that featured living sculptures of people with handkerchiefs covering their mouths. The idea was to challenge assumptions about which parts of the body can be displayed in public and which must remain hidden. Ono was at work on a companion piece, a film called *Bottoms,* which consisted of a series of stills of bare behinds.

LSD was initially confined to a small word-of-mouth culture; few outsiders had any idea what was going on. In the autumn of 1966 the jazz singer George Melly attended an exhibition of the work of Aubrey Beardsley at the Victoria and Albert Museum. Melly had always been a man of eccentric, even lonely, interests, and he expected to find an exhibition dedicated to an all but forgotten decadent artist who had briefly shocked Victorian London deserted. Instead he found it thronged and that everyone present was under twenty-five. Something was stirring underground, he realized.

In the early summer of 1967 London woke up and discovered it had acquired a counterculture, and Jimi, who had had little do with it so far, was one of its emblems.

Jimi had come across LSD in New York and tripped with Linda Keith, who recalls him as nervous about it and not sure whether LSD and acid were the same thing. In London any inhibitions he might have had were soon forgotten, and he tripped with Brian Jones, whom he had met through Kathy. Unlike other London guitarists, Jones' admiration for Jimi was not crossed with any sense of rivalry. Jones was among the first who heard the acetates of *Are You Experienced?* and he was full of encouragement and admiration.

backbiters and syndicators

Are You Experienced? was finally released at the end of the second week of May. Kit Lambert and Chris Stamp had originally planned to release it in March, a bold move because album sales were supposed to be driven by success in the singles chart. After "Hey Joe's" slow rise into the charts, "Purple Haze" had been released at the end of March, almost as soon as it was completed, and had reached number three in the Top Ten. The Experience's third single, "The Wind Cries Mary," was released simultaneously with *Are You Experienced?*

The release had been delayed because the project was frequently overtaken by the speed with which Jimi was producing new material, and delayed because Chas was learning to produce as he went along and mixed and remixed, not always sure of what he was trying to accomplish. An album by an artist just discovering his voice and a producer still finding his feet was hardly likely to be a statement of any kind, but in the climate of the time it could not escape being taken for one.

An anonymous reviewer in the *Melody Maker* was bemused but encouraging: "One of the most pleasing aspects of Jimi Hendrix's success is his refusal to be blatantly commercial. Subsequently the more 'real' Hendrix we hear the more commercial it becomes. Subsequently with *Are You Experienced?* we're getting the real Hendrix, and although it might seem weird and freaky to some, at least you can be sure it is, repeat is, the real Hendrix Experience."

To read that on Thursday, when the *Melody Maker* came out, and then go out and buy *Are You Experienced?* on the following Saturday, when you had time off from work or school, was an adventure and an act of trust. Albums, still referred to as LPs, usually delivered the familiar: more of the same from an act that had established itself through the singles chart. You bought *Are You Experienced?* with no expectation of enjoying it at the first play and no guarantee that you would come to like it all. You handed over your nineteen shillings and sixpence and hoped Jimi knew what he was doing and was not taking you for a ride.

Naturally there were those who thought the emperor had no clothes. Tony Palmer, pop music critic for London's oldest Sunday newspaper, the *Observer,* was unimpressed. "Owes everything to Cream," he wrote. "over laden with electronic effects, confuses gimmick with invention. One song hardly distinguishable from the next, and all characterised by moaning, groaning, and sobbing. Mostly out of tune and probably out of time. But much respected in the pop world because they are so 'meaningful'."

a hint of voodoo

Even the *Financial Times,* that somber, stuffy newspaper aimed at bankers and businessmen, felt it should take a position. At the end of the year, Michael Wale summarized the Summer of Love for his stockbroker readership:

> Drug taking for a time became fashionable. The Beatles admitted to having experienced LSD. It was the year of the big "turn on". Pop lyrics had begun to simulate LSD trips and being high on marijuana

and, with the use of flashing lights onstage, so did the groups. The leading exponents of this particular second hand freneticism were The Jimi Hendrix Experience.

Hendrix brought something new if only it was his incredible hair style which stood on end and looked as if he'd just touched the electric mains which fed his guitar.

Hendrix with a wild, untamed guitar sound and only another guitarist and his drummer for accompaniment, filled the role vacated by the Rolling Stones. There was a hint of voodoo about the group's music as "Hey Joe" "Purple Haze" and "Burning of the Midnight Oil" [sic] soared up the charts, rather bizarrely because the Hendrix tunes had no fixed shape and certainly no commercial sound. Presumably with the general acceptance by the adult population of all their heroes from The Monkees to The Beatles young people needed a point of musical revolt and try as hard as The Rolling Stones did, it was Hendrix who provided it in 1967.

It was correct to write of the Jimi Hendrix Experience as a "group" rather than as a single virtuoso. "Hey Joe" was built on Chas's ideas rather than Jimi's, and Jimi all but disowned the record as his own ideas took shape. But the smartest thing that the *Financial Times*' critic had to say was to ask why these records were hits at all.

"No fixed shape" is not entirely accurate. "Red House," which appeared on the British version of *Are You Experienced?* but not on the U.S. album released by Warner Brothers, is a deeply conventional twelve-bar blues. Yet the singles had no recognizable shape and eschewed the formula of hook, chorus, and bridge that pop music was based on then and is based on now. After forty years of continuous play it is easy to forget that Jimi's music was strange when it first emerged, and what is strange can also be forbidding and menacing.

Where Michael Wale is wildly wrong is in his supposition that *Are You Experienced?* is intentionally forbidding and menacing and that Jimi's music was an "anti-music," deliberately ugly and confrontational—music made so that it could not be co-opted as entertainment by mainstream society and would instead forever remain a shibboleth of the counterculture.

Not that the counterculture was sure about Jimi. At the other end of the cultural and political spectrum from the *Financial Times* was the *International Times*, London's underground newspaper dedicated to psychedelic revolution.

The newspaper of London's counterculture began to appear at bimonthly intervals at the end of 1966. Edited by a committee, it chose to expand its readers' consciousness through cold print rather than hot graphics. Behind the beautiful cover art work were densely printed articles pursuing philosophical points. The style was that of a Leninist journal rather than a comic book, and much space was dedicated to international news.

"The LP [*Are You Experienced?*] is definitely worth listening to, even if you are not a Hendrix fan, to see what advances are being made in this realm of music," concluded a brief review, signed "Dick, Vick, Richard." In other words, *International Times* readers should listen to Jimi, whether they liked it or not, as an educational exercise.

Jimi was an experimental musician but he was not an iconoclastic one. His ideas of what music is were naturalistic. His music stirs deep passions but there is nothing anarchic in it. He was not reaching out for chaos but attempting to awaken something within. He believed music could change people but that change would awaken dormant potential rather than shatter everything, leaving it to be remade anew.

"We were interested, Jimi and I," recalls Roger Mayer,

> in taking someone on a space journey—it would take them out, the sound of the guitars. It's well known that if you hit the right notes on the guitar, the right

sound on the guitar, it's got sexual connotations for women, it's got rock and roll, it's got power, it's got all kinds of stuff. But that's historical; lots of people cleverer than I have written books about it, whether its martial music, or military music or whatever. And it comes from the Church, it goes through choral music, it goes through chants, all sorts of stuff you can follow how various people have used sounds and environments for different purposes.

It was with Roger that Jimi shared his underlying ideas.

We just used to chat about it, like we are now. And we'd say, "Oh that's interesting." The idea really is to paint a picture with the sound that takes somebody on a journey. And if you do that with a classical symphony or with rock and roll, and you get it right, it's an enduring thing. And the interesting thing is that if you get it right, it's perceived universally. Jimi's not the only artist I've worked with. I've worked with Bob Marley and a lot of people. And when you get the quality of the sound right, it internationally travels, because it's all about sounding good. If I said to you that sounds good, you could be uneducated, you could be in Africa or Chinese—[but] if you get the sound right you're going to hit some primitive, or whatever you want to call it, chord inside the person.

Noel, Jimi, and Mitch touch down on their return to London from the Monterey Festival in 1967.

chapter 11

a little help from my friends

a day in the life

In June 1967 Paul McCartney turned twenty-five. It is possible that no young man had enjoyed such fame, wealth, and influence as he basked in that summer since the days of Alexander the Great.

A side view into McCartney's life at this time is given in the diaries of the playwright Joe Orton. In January 1967 Orton was on the point of being commissioned to write the script of the third Beatles movie. The movie was a contractual obligation that the Beatles were reluctant to fulfill and were eventually to wriggle out of through the feature-length cartoon, *Yellow Submarine*. While it was still a live project, Orton was a natural but also a bold a choice as writer. A youthful thirty-four, from a working-class family in the Midlands town of Leicester, he wrote camp and knowing black comedies and was just the writer to scrape off the sugar coating *A Hard Day's Night* and *Help!* had spun around the Beatles. For his part, Orton was a fiercely independent man, enjoying a West End hit after years of penury. Intrigued as he was by the Beatles movie, he had no need for Beatle money, and embarked on the project with detached amusement.

He took a bus to **(25) Chapel Street**, Belgravia, to meet McCartney in a house owned by the Beatles' manager.

Arrived in Belgravia at ten minutes to eight having caught a 19 bus which dropped me at Hyde Park Corner. I found Chapel Street easily. I rang the bell and an old man opened the door. He seemed surprised to see me. "Is this Brian Epstein's house?" I said. "Yes, sir," he said, and led the way into the hall. I suddenly realized that the man was the butler. I've never seen one before. He took my coat and I went to the lavatory. When I came out he'd gone. There was nobody about. I wandered around a large dining-room which was laid for dinner. And then I got to feel strange. The house appeared to be empty. So I went upstairs to the first floor. I heard music only I couldn't decide where it came from. So I went up a further flight of stars. I found myself in a bedroom. I came down again and found the butler. He took me into a room and said in a loud voice "Mr Orton". Everybody looked up and stood to their feet. I was introduced to one or two people. And Paul McCartney. He was just as the photographs. Only he'd grown a moustache. His hair was shorter too. He was playing the latest Beatles recording, "Penny Lane". I liked it very much. Then he played the other side—Strawberry something. I didn't like this as much. We talked intermittently. Before we went down to dinner we'd thrown out the idea of setting the film in the thirties. We went down to dinner. The crusted old retainer—looking too much like a butler to be good casting—busied himself in the corner. "The only thing I get from the theatre," Paul M. said, "is a sore arse." He said *Loot* was the only play he hadn't wanted to leave before the end. "I'd have liked a bit more," he said. We talked of drugs, of mushrooms which give hallucinations—like LSD. "The drug not the money," I said. We talked of tattoos. And, after one or two veiled references, marijuana. I said I'd smoked it in Morocco. The atmosphere relaxed a little. Dinner ended and we went upstairs again. We watched a programme on TV. It had phrases in it like "in-crowd", and "swinging London." There was a little scratching at the door. I thought it was the old retainer, but someone got up to open the door and about five very young and pretty boys trooped in. I rather hope this was the evening's entertainments. It wasn't though. It was a pop group called The Easybeats. I'd seen them on TV. I liked them very much then. In a way they were better (or prettier) off stage than on. After awhile Paul McCartney said "Let's go upstairs." So he and I and Peter Brown went upstairs to a room also fitted with a TV. A French photographer arrived with two beautiful youths and a girl. He'd taken a set of new photographs of The Beatles. They wanted one to use on their new Record sleeve. Excellent photograph. And the four Beatles look different with their moustaches. Like anarchists in the early years of the century. After awhile we went downstairs. The Easybeats still there. The girl went away. I talked to the leading Easybeat. Feeling slightly like an Edwardian masher with a Gaiety Girl. And then came over all tired and decided to go home. I had a last word with Paul M. "Well," I said, "I'd like to do the film. There's only one thing we've got to fix up." "You mean the bread?" "Yes." We smiled and parted. I got a cab home. It was pissing down.

the beatles machine

Although the dinner was hosted in Brian Epstein's house, Orton makes no mention of Epstein himself. Both Orton and McCartney assumed that any creative decisions were McCartney's alone. McCartney was lucky in his manager, or rather they were lucky in each other. Epstein had stumbled into the music business through the Beatles. He did not have the calculation of Mike Jefferies or even the business acumen of Kit Lambert and Chris Stamp, who had taken time to study how breakfast cereals were marketed before they set up Track Records. Epstein had risen from managing the record department in his father's department store to managing the world's first supergroup in less than five years.

Yet, despite his lack of his experience, he was a fundamentally good businessman and had built a network of enterprises around the success of the Beatles. He was fundamentally a kind-hearted man, too, and respected his artists. He was happy to let McCartney pull the levers on the Beatles machine.

It is a grim coincidence that before the Summer of Love was out, both Joe Orton and Brian Epstein would be dead, Orton murdered by his lover, Epstein killed by his own hand.

rise and shine

One of Epstein's many enterprises were Sunday evening concerts at the **(26) Saville Theatre**, 135-149 Shaftesbury Avenue. The Saville Theatre had been built in 1930 at the eastern end of Shaftesbury Avenue, London's theatre strip, but on the fringe of theatreland on the other side of Charing Cross Road, and the opposite end from Piccadilly Circus, the heart of nighttime London, where Joe Orton's *Loot* was playing at the Criterion Theatre. In the summer of 1967 Spike Milligan's *The Bed Sitting Room* was playing at the Saville. Noel went to see it on a night off, and managed to talk his way back stage, where he found Milligan, seated cross-legged on his dressing room floor like a guru. "Got anything to smoke?" he asked Noel.

It was during a Sunday evening concert at the Saville Theatre that Jimi pulled off one of his great *coups de theatre*. On the first Sunday of June, the Experience were top of the bill, and the 1,200-seat theatre was full, with people still arriving to be turned away at the door. Jimi's opening number was "Sgt. Pepper's Lonely Hearts Club

Band," which had been released only three days previously. Paul Mc-Cartney, who was in the audience, was deeply impressed.

"It's still obviously a shining memory for me, because I admired him so much anyway, he was so accomplished," he told his official biographer, Barry Miles, in 1997.

> To think that that album meant so much to him as to actually do it by the Sunday night, three days after the release. He must have been so into it, because normally it might take a day for rehearsal and then you might wonder whether you'd put it in, but he just opened with it. It's a pretty major compliment in anyone's book. I put that down as one of the great honors of my career. I'm sure he wouldn't have thought of it as an honor, I'm sure he thought it was the other way round, but to me that was like a great boost.

Jimi, Noel, and Mitch did not need a day to rehearse a new song; all three were used to learning entire sets in an hour or two. Jimi had walked into the dressing room at the Saville that night with a copy of *Sgt. Pepper*, played the first track, and told Mitch and Noel it would be their opening number. There was no hesitation; it was a calculated attempt to upstage the Beatles.

"It was never a question of can we do it? Or how much is this going to cost?" recalls Roger Mayer. "With Jimi it was 'Let's do it.' Whatever it takes we're going to do it. Let's be on the edge. Let's be on the cutting edge. That was the whole premise behind it. Let's blow some fucking minds here. So Jimi would get up at the Saville Theatre and the Beatles are there: 'Let's play Sgt. Pepper for them.' What do you think of that?"

Paul had been one of the first to see Jimi play in London when all four Beatles had attended the press launch at the Bag O'Nails. His enthusiasm was close to evangelistic, and he was to be directly responsible for the next leap in Jimi's career.

In early months of 1967, Paul's girlfriend, the actress Jane Asher, had been away in the United States touring in a play.

Paul, who found theatre a literal pain in the arse, could not see why she should wish to continue to pursue her vocation. Kathy, who at the age of twenty-one could not see why anyone should work when they did not have to, would sympathize with his point of view when Paul complained about Jane's absence.

In April Paul flew from London to Boulder, Colorado, to surprise Jane on the last night of her tour. He went via Los Angeles, to pick up the private jet in which he would complete the last stage of the journey. During his LA stopover he met up with the members of Jefferson Airplane. He played them one of the first pressings of *Sgt. Pepper,* jammed a little, and sang Jimi's praises. It was due to Paul's enthusiasm that Jimi and the Experience were invited to play at an open air festival to be held in the fairgrounds at Monterey, just over a hundred miles south of San Francisco, that summer.

Before leaving for California, Jimi repaid the favor by agreeing to play on an album being recorded by Paul's brother, Mike McGear, and Roger McGough. McGear and McGough were poets—and two-thirds of the comedy trio called the Scaffold—and the idea for the album was to have them read their witty, self-effacing poems about ordinary life in Liverpool against a sophisticated musical backdrop provided by the Experience and the Spencer Davis Group, among others. In the event, the two poets found themselves as provincial bystanders in the middle of an extraordinary three-day jamming session. The resulting record was not a commercial success.

chapter 12

the color
of sound

summer in the city

The summer of 1967 in London blazes in the memory of those who can recall it. Memory notoriously colors the past, but those who remember it is as a literally brilliant summer are not deceiving themselves. When Joe Orton returned from a summer holiday in Morocco he noted in his diary that London felt hotter than Marrakesh.

Within a week of Jimi's return to London in August, the Flower-Power Generation suffered its first trace of blight. While Jimi and the Experience were performing at the Saville Theatre on the last Sunday of August, news came that Brian Epstein had been found dead from a barbiturate overdose at his country house. It was a public holiday weekend. The Beatles were away together in Wales on a meditation retreat led by Mahesh Yogi, who styled himself the "Maharishi." From LSD to Indian mysticism in a few short months—the Beatles' experience personified the challenges that were arising to society's understanding of reality itself, and the pace with which they were arriving. These spiritual and cultural caprices came and then went, as fads do in a city hungry for novelty, yet each seemed potentially earth-shattering.

The two months Jimi had been away from London had been fast-paced too. In the short term, his excursion to California had been timely. "Jimi's work permit was on its last legs" Noel recalls. In the long term, the trip made musical history. At the now legendary Monterey Festival, the Experience, together with the Who, had introduced the audience to the anarchic and Dionysian side of Swinging London. The Who smashed television sets; Jimi set light to his guitar. Both performances were a gift to the movie cameras recording the event, and the subsequent movie introduced Jimi to audiences across the United States—and created certain expectations of him, too.

From Monterey, the Experience went to San Francisco, initially to support Jefferson Airport at the Fillmore Theater. When the Airplane discovered that they could not play to an audience whipped up into a state of excitement by Jimi, the Experience took over as the main act.

Then, to their astonishment and dismay, the Experience were booked to support the Monkees on an East Coast tour. The Monkees' audience had little patience with experimental rock music, and indeed little time for any band that was not the Monkees. Even if they had been more open-minded, Jimi would have made little impression on them, because the Experience, very likely the loudest band in the world at that time, could not make themselves heard above the roar of a stadium packed with excited teenage girls.

the light fantastic

When Jimi returned to London that summer, the struggle to establish himself was over. The Experience no longer lived a hand-to-mouth existence that depended on constant gigging to keep going financially. Success in London with the promise of more success in the United States had prompted Mike Jeffries to muscle his way back into his partnership with Chas. One consequence was that Jimi, Noel, and Mitch were able to draw petty cash from Mike's offices in Gerrard Street as they pleased.

With more time on his hands than before, Jimi had the chance to delve deeper into the counterculture scene that had co-opted him as a figurehead. He began with a club that was literally underground. **(27) UFO**, 31 Tottenham Court Road, always pronounced you-foe, had opened its doors at the very end of 1966. It had been founded by John Hopkins, who earned his living as a freelance photographer but devoted his energies to connecting up the various threads—political, utopian, psychedelic—that were weaving together to form underground London, and Joe Boyd, born in Cambridge, Massachusetts, who had come to London as an A&R man for Elektra Records and was striking out on his own as an independent record producer.

At the junction where Tottenham Court Road meets Oxford Street, the multistoried mausoleum-like Centre Point was rising, an office block built of white concrete and glass. London's most striking tall building, the thin, round GPO Tower, was visible over the rooftops, but much of Tottenham Court Road was made up of two- or three-story buildings, many fronted by modest shops selling electrical equipment. It was here that Joe Boyd found the Blarney Club, an Irish dance hall, in basement premises between two cinemas. Its proprietor, Joe Gannon, was prepared to let it out overnight on Fridays to Saturdays provided he kept the soft drink concession. Beneath the mirrored lights that passed for formal elegance in the 1960s, underground London found its first public meeting place.

Mark Boyle, who ran light shows at UFO with his wife, Joan Hills, has left this account of the nights there:

> A typical evening at UFO would begin around 10.30 to 11.00 with Vivaldi very loud on the sound system and our light environment all around the room. Then, when the place was full, the first rock group would appear. Then you might get a theatre group from the Royal Court Theatre doing mime, followed by the Soft Machine or the Pink Floyd.
>
> Then I might be asked to make yellow projections while the current hit Mellow Yellow would be played

and David Medalla and a group of dancers would fill an arena with more and more yellow objects, yellow cloth, yellow confetti, yellow paint etc. A folk group would follow, then a clown, more rock, more Bach, a theatre group called the People's Show and then at about 7 a.m. a jazz group called the Sun Trolley would play. Most people would be sleeping against the pillars or in little piles on the floor by now. Usually it was just the Sun Trolley and Joan and I who were awake. Then we would go away and get some breakfast.

UFO was more than a nightclub; it brought a sense of community to people who believed themselves to be spiritual and social pioneers, discovering new ways of being for themselves as individuals or for society at large. It also became the meeting place for anyone who wanted to influence that community. The corridor between the bar and the dance floor became cluttered with tables displaying leaflets for radical causes, the most prominent cause being reform of the drug laws. John Hopkins became a cause in his own right when he was jailed for possession of cannabis in June.

The original house band at UFO was Pink Floyd. Joe Boyd had produced their first single "Arnold Layne" before they were signed to EMI and taken out of his hands. As Pink Floyd's touring schedule took off on the back of the improbable chart success of "Arnold Layne," they were replaced by the Soft Machine, a Kent-based, art school band committed to the then unlikely project of rock and jazz fusion. Taking their name from a William S. Burroughs novel, there was little danger of them being sucked away into the mainstream.

Jimi was impressed, and came to jam with them several times during the autumn of 1967. He also was deeply impressed by the Boyle family's light show. Generally, the Boyles were secretive about their techniques; imitations of their work were springing up across Europe. But whenever they played the Speakeasy, which was only a few streets away from UFO, Jimi was allowed to sit beside Joan at the control panel and watch her work.

acid vision

Jimi was very interested in the relationship between music and color. With little or no formal education in music to speak of (he had got an F in the subject at high school), Jimi thought about music in terms of colors. "He talked in colors when it came to sounds," says Roger Mayer, "when it came to the emotions and the sounds. Most of the people who are involved in sound that I know of . . . tend to talk in colors, because if you can't form in your own mind a visual picture of it, what can you do? Talking about sound is a paradox in itself so you have to use visual terms."

Synaesthetic experiences, where sounds acquire vivid and specific associations with colors, are common occurrences during LSD trips. Jimi was taking a good deal of LSD during the autumn of 1967. Chas subsequently discovered he was dropping a tab a day at this time. One of the curious properties of LSD is that, above a certain level, an increase of the dose will have no further effect on the user. As small a dose as 250 micrograms is enough for a mild acid trip, a dose double that will be stronger, but tripling the dose will barely have any effect beyond that. Frequent LSD use will create resistance to the drug, but it is not like the cumulative resistance built up by heroin use that can be overcome by larger and larger doses.

Daily LSD use is unlikely to have much if any physical effect, but LSD is a drug of the mind and the environment, and in a suitable environment the mind can be trained to revisit episodes of LSD experience (so called "flashbacks"). Re-encountering LSD experiences is apt to encourage the idea that synaesthetic connections between color and sound are not personal associations but glimpses into an underlying reality. In the rush of academic excitement that surrounded the emergence of LSD, far better educated minds' than Jimi's allowed themselves to be seduced by this proposition. Jimi, who was barely educated, would be fascinated by the relationship between sound and color for the rest of his short life.

Jeremy Thorpe, a member of Parliament, tries out Jimi's Flying V backstage at the Royal Festival Hall. The BBC had only recently relaxed the rule that its radio presenters must change into evening dress after 6 p.m., so formal conventions such as evening dress accompanied the experimental excesses of Swinging London.

chapter 13

one hundred seconds of magic

the sophomore album

October was set aside to record the Experience's second album. *Axis Bold as Love* is usually dismissed by critics as the Experience's "sophomore album." Yet even after they had recorded what is widely considered their finest album, *Electric Ladyland,* Roger, Noel, and Jimi himself still judged *Axis* to be the Experience's best work in the studio.

"*Axis Bold as Love,* that was the album for me, because it really encapsulated the period and it sounds like a proper album," Roger says now.

> I think because we had more time to set aside to record it and it wasn't recorded on the fly in between gigs like the first album.
>
> *Are You Experienced?* was a bit cobbled together, shall we say? It's not as cohesive as that one. And *Electric Ladyland*...shows [Jimi's] frustration at not having the

right people around him. Although it's got a few blinding tracks on it, it didn't come together in the same way.

By modern standards *Axis* was recorded very swiftly, in about sixteen days of studio time. This was still a fortnight too long as far as Noel was concerned. A barnstormer by instinct as well as by background, he was impatient with the constant finessing the studio required. He spent much of the studio time in the pub across the road, waiting to be called to put down his bass part. The more time he spent in the pub the more suspicious he became that Jimi was putting down the bass lines behind his back.

Chas and Jimi quarreled over Jimi's acid use. "I told him he had to be straight some of the time," Chas was to recall. "I thought it would give him a new slant to his lyrics but he'd lose his temper." The overall mood in the studio was highly positive, however, as Roger recalls:

> When we came out the studio, we had a good feeling about it. I don't think there was much doubt in our mind, we felt good about it. Jimi understood, much like many other artists I've worked with, who are very in tune, what you're struggling for is a couple hundred of seconds of magic or [even] less than twenty seconds, and it takes many, many things to do that. It takes the right food, the right sandwiches, the right environment—you have to gear in the whole day to get it right, thirty seconds of solo. It's an art form, isn't it?

One of Noel's songs, "She's So Fine," was included on the album. This was a financial bonus as well as a career boost, because Noel would receive a small royalty from each pressing. The initiative to include Noel and Mitch in the publishing credits came solely from Jimi. Mitch chose not exercise the option.

When it was time for Jimi and Mitch to record the backing vocals for "She's So Fine," Jimi became helpless with laughter. Such laughing fits took hold of him from time to time, and they were bewildering and embarrassing for onlookers. The fits were so strong that Jimi could not talk through them. If they began with a secret joke which had flickered across his mind, they became a great outburst of joie de vivre.

painting soundscapes

There was more time for experimentation in the studio than there had been during the recording of *Are You Experienced?* and Jimi's writing technique changed accordingly: songs began to grow out of jamming sessions and sound effects devised by Roger. The songs for *Are You Experienced?* were tried out and improved in front of live audiences. The all new material for *Axis Bold as Love*, already expected by the record label within four months of the release of the first album, grew out of play.

Olympic Studios now had eight-track recording machines, and Jimi and Mitch enjoyed recording comedy routines on them, including the playful short track that opens *Axis*.

Roger's experiments fed into the creative process. "Put it this way," Roger says,

> which comes first? If you don't have the device to change the sound you can't write the song because Jimi would take the sound into his own mind and make it his, he'd own it. You don't just come along and add the effects afterwards. You can't do it. The song has got to be written with the sound.
>
> The techniques we were using in the studio were very cutting edge. We were getting as much movement and change in texture of the sound as we could. Painting a very nice soundscape for the people.

dream trips

If the music was to some extent a collaboration, the lyrics were very much Jimi's. Traces of Bob Dylan's imagist writing linger on *Axis,* but Dylan was by now an inescapable influence for any songwriter. The images Jimi paints are his own. There are flourishes of traditional blues lyrics—the protests to Dolly Mae in "Wait Until Tomorrow," for example. Yet there is an almost mediaeval visionary quality that is very much Jimi's own. It is drawn, so the words themselves declare, from dream and dreams of color, just as the original inspiration for "Purple Haze" had been.

Some of the ideas expressed are obviously autobiographical. The Spanish Castle in "Spanish Castle Magic" was the name of a dance hall just outside of Seattle. The Indian boy playing in the woods in "Castles Made of Sand" is a fragment of Jimi's childhood and not necessarily an idealized fragment either. The couple who argue in the street in the first verse of the same song are an echo of Jimi and Kathy's explosive public quarrels.

Many listeners have assumed that the woman in "Little Wing," the album's best-known song, is Jimi's mother. Vague as the hints are either way, she seems to be more an idealized vision of the feminine, which includes unconditional mother love. There is nothing particularly maternal in the picture the first verse presents of a woman lost in happy abstraction. The unhappy girl who watches the golden ship of opportunity pass her by from her wheelchair in "Castles Made of Sand" seems closer to the unfortunate Norah Hendrix.

Chas played the final mix to Jimi, Noel, and Mitch on October 30. The following night Jimi borrowed both master reels to take to a party and left one behind in his taxi home. Chas and Eddie Kramer returned to Olympic Studios and reconstructed the missing side overnight.

The cover art was commissioned by Kit Lambert and came as a disappointment to Jimi. The project was given to Roger Law, who was to be one of the two artists who established the political puppet show Spitting Image in the 1980s. The design took on a Hindu theme, on the back of the Maharishi's influence. Jimi, Noel, and Mitch appeared as three faces of a mock Hindu deity, with Jimi as the center. The idea behind the design did at least recognize the Experience as an entity rather than as Jimi and his sidemen. Jimi hated it on first sight. "I ain't that kind of Indian," he said. His management were blunter still. "There was a big row over the cover," Chas recalled. "Mike thought it was crap." Nevertheless, the design went ahead.

chapter 14

the road to excess

In the middle of November Jimi set off on the biggest tour he would ever make in Britain. Less than six months after he had appeared toward the bottom of the bill on the Walker Brothers farewell tour, he was top of the bill of a roster of flower-power chart bands that included Pink Floyd and the Move. The tour began in London at the enormous Albert Hall.

bacchanalia

Behind the scenes on that first night, Chas calmed the performers' nerves with scotch and Coca-Cola. As the tour rolled out through the provinces, the backstage areas descended into hysterical bacchanalia, with the young women of Britain everywhere eager and obliging when they could talk their way past the stage door and ferociously predatory en masse outside the theatres.

Nick Mason, Pink Floyd's drummer, was terrified and appalled. The year before, he had been an architecture student at London Central Polytechnic, one of the students who had jostled his way to see Cream's debut concert there. He still considered Pink Floyd's extraordinary success a sabbatical from college. The success had been extraordinary in every sense of the word, with a chart hit about an underwear fetishist (banned by the BBC), a short tour of the United States, and the still unrecognized psychotic breakdown of the band's singer and guitarist, Syd Barrett (nicknamed Laughing Syd by Jimi for his near-catatonic gloom). None of these experiences shook Mason so much as the predatory female sexuality he encountered touring with the Experience. Nick Mason, engaged to his teenage sweetheart who he was to marry, fled, and still remembers the sound of a thunder of high heels as he was chased down a side street in a northern town.

Extreme crowd behavior generated extreme crowd control. The provincial cities of Britain have always been tougher than London, and provincial venues fielded some truly alarming security men. In Newcastle one security man took a blow to his head with an axe and still managed to knock down all eight of his assailants. Then he walked to the local hospital to have the wound treated.

the queen of ears

The frantic sexual activity, which ended in an epidemic of gonorrhea, did not undermine Jimi's relationship with Kathy. She understood that he depended on her for a sense of domestic security. She could not resist a sardonic satisfaction at the dismay Jimi felt when other women pursued him. Jimi hated to say no to anyone about anything, and his only strategy to escape groupies who hoped for more than a one-night stand was to change his telephone number.

Kathy had taken some lessons in cookery from Ronnie Money and mastered the Scottish dish of mince and tatties (ground beef and mashed or boiled potatoes). As a birthday surprise she brought Jimi a dog, a female basset hound who was named Ethel Floon but who Jimi always called the Queen of Ears. Itinerant and mostly homeless for all his adult life, Jimi had long dreamed of owning a dog. Clumsy and untrainable as bassets are, Ethel lived an indulged life, walked in Hyde Park by Kathy and forgiven for her lapses in toilet training.

Nightclubs were as much a part of Jimi and Kathy's domestic life as ever, and the jazz club Ronnie Scott's became a favorite hangout, not least for its opportunities for late-night jams. **(28) Ronnie Scott's Club**, 47 Frith Street, was and still is London's most prestigious jazz venue. This unpretentious nightclub has accommodated most of the major names in jazz over the past half-century. In the 1960s, musicians' unions of both sides of the Atlantic restricted the number of foreign acts who could perform in their respective countries, but Ronnie Scott's still brought over musicians who were making their mark on the history of jazz, such as the trumpeter Dizzy Gillespie and the pianist Cecil Taylor, pioneers, respectively, of bebop and free jazz.

the king of ears

In November 1967 Jimi met a fellow African American musician at Ronnie Scott's who was to become an influence and a mentor. Like Jimi, Roland Kirk was a musician whose showmanship distracted audiences from his virtuosity, and his performances were often dismissed as gimmickry.

He was born in Columbus, Ohio, in 1936 and became blind at the age of two. He set his heart on becoming a musician at the age of eight when he discovered the bugle at a Boy Scout camp. As a teenager he had a dream that he was playing three saxophones at once. He was determined to follow this inspiration up, and through the discovery of two obscure brass reed instruments, the manzello and the stritch, he made the dream a reality when he played both together with his tenor sax.

His approach to the flute was also radical as he adapted African techniques to the European instrument and hummed and groaned through it. In his recordings and his performances he incorporated nonmusical sounds such as sirens and police whistles. Part of Roland's flute technique was to bring the instrument and the human voice closer together, so that the flute apparently mimicked phrases of human speech. This was an idea Jimi was to apply to his guitar, and he learned to make it sound a few phrases very close to "Thank you, thank you" in acknowledgement of applause.

As a blind performer, engaging with the audience was important to Kirk. He was not content with hearing applause, he appeared to feel the atmosphere he created. He liked audience participation and sometimes handed out whistles to all present. Like Jimi again, Kirk's music was deeply rooted in the blues. With their mutual interest in electronic sounds, plus their shared conviction on the merits of LSD, a friendship was bound to spring up.

The last edition of *Melody Maker* for 1967 carried a special front cover illustrated by Viv Stanshall of the Bonzo Dog Doo Dah Band. At the hub of a circle of cartoons and scribbled in-jokes was a large image of Jimi gazing into a crystal ball. The implication was clear, and astonishingly coherent for anything that emerged from Stanshall's unusual mind: As the kaleidoscopic year of 1967 receded, it was plain that it had belonged Jimi, and that if anybody understood what challenging mysteries 1968 would hold, it must be him.

Jimi's thoughts of his immediate future were focused on the United States. Success in America was thought to be the natural progression for any successful British pop band. Jimi's conquest of Britain was often seen as American retaliation for the British invasion of the *Billboard* charts. For Jimi, success in his own country was a far more meaningful quest than an attempt to follow the trail blazed by the Beatles.

On his way to Monterey, Jimi had looked up old friends in Harlem, who had taken his tales of his life in London as acid-fuelled fantasy. From the perspective of New York, and especially from that of Harlem, where there was no interest in British pop culture, Jimi's success appeared illusory.

It seemed to Noel that as soon as Jimi returned to London after his triumphs in California, all his ambitions centered on the United States. Those ambitions were encouraged by Mike Jefferies, who had already conquered America once with the Animals and was eager to build on what he had learned. Once *Axis* was released, Jimi began building his American war party. Roger was invited to join—as a thank you for his unpaid work on the album—and accepted on condition that he didn't have to carry any amps or deal with Jimi's managers. Mark Boyle and Joan Hills were invited to take their light show on the road, but decided that their loyalties lay with Soft Machine

Underground London finished 1967 with a three-day celebration called Christmas on Earth held at the vast **(29) Olympia Exhibition Hall**, Hammersmith Road, near Earls Court in West London, originally built in the 1920s to stage circuses. Jimi and the Experience were a major attraction at what was a chaotic event. Noel carried away a vivid memory of the occasion. "I encountered strobe lights for the first time. I got lost in them, feeling far too detached, but I knew I had to play. All I could see were old-time movie flickers of Jimi laughing at me as I tried to keep in touch with the tempo. I still can't handle strobes. Everything was designed to let it 'flow', but it was sometimes hard not just to melt away."

An anti–Vietnam War protestor confronts a mounted policeman near the U.S. Embassy in Grosvenor Square in 1968. Not everybody in London believed that all you need is love.

chapter 15

the angry year

time to split

In the late spring of 1968 Chas came back from the United States unexpectedly early and alone. He arrived at Upper Berkeley Street and told Kathy that he and Jimi's relationship was over. The immediate implication of this for Kathy was that she was homeless with no income of her own. In the heat of the moment, Chas gave her to understand that this was her problem.

With no idea of Jimi's income to work with, Kathy approached rental agencies and found that central London landlords were reluctant to rent to Jimi Hendrix or any other pop star. To put pressure on her to move, Chas booked a double room for her and Jimi in a hotel in Earls Court. Kathy was crestfallen at the prospect of returning to the bed-sit land she had lived in as a teenager. She was horrified when she inspected the premises and found a bare, dirty room with two iron bedsteads, no bathroom, and a payphone in the hall.

She complained to her friend Carol, who was then living with Graham Edge, drummer for the Moody Blues, in a small Bayswater flat that they shared with the band's guitarist, Justin Hayward.

Going through the London evening papers together, Kathy and Carol found a flat privately advertised at **(30) 23 Brook Street**, in Mayfair, above a restaurant called Mr. Love. The landlord was the restaurateur. When warned about who his tenants were, he smiled and said he did not care as long as the rent was paid. The rent was £30 a week, which Kathy felt was expensive, and it was twice what it would have cost to rent a bed-sit.

musical differences

Kathy never found out either from Chas or from Jimi why they fell out. Both refused to discuss the subject with her. In a 1972 interview Chas claimed that Jimi had become rebellious, if not entirely out of control. "There were a few heavy incidents. He smashed up a hotel in Sweden and hit a girl in Los Angeles. He smashed up two cars in one week in LA. He went through a weird period. He wouldn't listen to anybody. He was tearing himself apart for no apparent reason. I wasn't wanted anymore so I split and flew back to England."

Jimi had been arrested in Sweden for damage to his hotel room during a short tour in early 1968. It was only due to Lotta's family connections that he did not get into serious trouble. He could, when drunk, be violent with women. His auto wrecks were due to his refusal to wear glasses when driving, rather than his being out of control.

The truth was not that Jimi was refusing to listen to anyone but that he had been listening carefully to Mike Jefferies.

It would be wrong to jump to the conclusion that Jefferies' interest in Jimi was entirely mercenary. As Jimi's recording sessions became more crowded with hangers-on Mike was tempted to try and influence their artistic content, however ill equipped he was to make a contribution. He was at least interested in the music. Managing Jimi changed him and he came to believe that with Jimi he was on a mission to change human consciousness. This sense of higher purpose did nothing to alter his avaricious nature, but it did undermine his business judgment, to Jimi's cost financially, physically, and emotionally.

Jimi for his part was gaining confidence in the studio and no longer felt the need for Chas's assertive direction.

There is no doubt that Mike's strongest card in his own game to prize Jimi away from Chas, and under his sole control, was his financial expertise. During the U.S. tour Mike took Jimi aside and presented him with an inventive financial strategy to maximize Jimi's earnings, together with an ultimatum that Jimi must choose between Mike or Chas.

For Jimi the decision to reject Chas promised artistic independence in the short term and impossible riches in the long term. It is not surprising that he took it. Once he had, he lacked the moral courage to make a plain declaration and preferred to freeze Chas out. Like the adulterous partner in a marriage, Jimi worked to provoke Chas to leave him rather than walk out himself.

There was to be no clean break. Chas did not entirely give up on Jimi and the Experience until the end of 1968. His partnership with Mike was not formally dissolved until 1979, several years after Jefferies had died. He did feel, however, that he should claim the flat on Upper Berkeley Street for himself and thereby improve his relationship with Lotta.

at home in mr. love

The flat on Brook Street appealed to Kathy because it was on the top floor and to reach it one had to go through a narrow street door and up several flights of stairs. The arrangement would give Kathy the chance to vet visitors and keep out hangers-on and other nuisances without Jimi having to become involved.

Once she had agreed upon the rent, Kathy began to shop for furnishings for what would be her and Jimi's first and only home together. Preparations were not complete when Jimi arrived back from America at the end of May, and for a while they moved into the newly built **(31) Londonderry Hotel**, 19 Park Lane, opposite Hyde Park.

Kathy shared Jimi's love of patterned fabrics, and she fitted out the flat in the souk chic, carpets as wall hangings, and other patterned fabrics, that were fashionable at the time. A *Melody Maker* journalist who interviewed Jimi at Brook Street in early 1969 gave this description to his readers:

> A lifelike rubber rat stared at the TV in Jimi Hendrix's top floor flat just off London's Bond Street.
>
> A stuffed Panda sat on the floor wearing a green hat and what seemed to be a teddy bear in the last stages of malnutrition hung from a nail in the wall. Over the bed a Persian rug served as a canopy, giving the effect of a four poster. A large Roland Kirk type gong stood near the bed and most available surfaces were covered with guitars, assorted electronic equipment, transistor radios, a cine projector and a vase full of feathers.

Kathy and Jimi's sitting room doubled as a sound laboratory where Jimi worked with Roger, while Kathy passed the time reading magazines and keeping the world at bay.

war cries

Brook Street is just a few minutes' walk away from the United States Embassy in Grosvenor Square, which in 1968 was the center of much hostile attention. In March that year a ten thousand–strong protest march had ended with an unusually violent confrontation with the police. Two hundred protestors were arrested and fifty people injured seriously enough to require hospital treatment; half of these were police officers.

1968 was turning out to be an edgier year than 1967. Flower power had considered itself a devastating challenge to the status quo but had been taken as nothing more than a bizarre carnival by its onlookers. Now the underground was allying itself with traditional radicals and campaigning on concrete political issues. In March an international anarchist group set off several small bombs simultaneously in the capitals of Europe. (The London attempt, aimed at a U.S. officers' club in Lancaster Gate, failed to detonate.) In May the French government collapsed beneath a general strike and student protest in Paris. In another sign of the times, the more radical *Oz* magazine replaced the *International Times* as the house journal of the underground.

the underground from down under

Oz magazine had originally been founded in Australia in 1963 as a provocative irritant to a conservative society still in thrall to its colonial ties with Britain. When editors Richard Neville and Martin Sharp decided to transfer their activities to London, they were disappointed to find no radical press to speak of in the mother country. With no obvious collaborators to be found, Neville and Sharp decided to strike out on their own. Meanwhile they had discovered LSD. The discovery had its most profound effect on Sharp's role as art editor. *Oz* became an explosion of colorful graphics driven by an editorial line dedicated to hard-headed left-wing politics.

The major grievance against the United States and its embassy was the war in Vietnam. This was not an entirely vicarious cause for British youth. President Lyndon Johnson and the U.S. State Department were applying diplomatic pressure on Britain to involve itself in the war. There was already a contingent of Australian troops in Vietnam, and because Australia was still closely tied to Britain politically as well as culturally, it was not inconceivable that British troops would be deployed in Southeast Asia as they had been in Korea in the previous decade. Although Washington wanted no more than a token British force, the specter of conscription to fight an unjustified war inspired numerous demonstrations.

The protests commanded little widespread public support. The protestors were believed to be mostly students, and British students enjoyed a privileged life in the 1960s. University education was expanding, and British students suffered from none of the provocations that had inflamed student activism in Continental Europe: overcrowded classes, inadequate accommodation, and suffocating dorm rules.

It was also thought that the protests were orchestrated by Communists. There was some truth in this. The British Communist Party was a small organization, but it punched above its weight through its influence on the trade union movement, which was very strong in Britain in the 1960s. One of the leaders of the anti-Vietnam war movement was Hugh Scanlon, general secretary of the Electricians Union and a member of the Communist Party.

But most of the young people marching in the streets had no sympathy for a party that was little more than a lobby group for the foreign policy of the Soviet Union. After all, the stern-faced Soviet leaders were even more hostile to the spirit of youth than the most conservative old guards of Western Europe, as was proved when they crushed the liberalizing reform movement that emerged in Czechoslovakia.

Tucked away in their second-floor flat, Jimi and Kathy cared little about the political battles being fought below. "Sometimes the journalists would ask him questions about politics and race relations because Vietnam and the civil rights movement were in the news," Kathy recalls in her memoirs. "We hardly ever thought about these things. Jimi didn't seem to have any clear-cut political ideas, just a vague belief that everyone should try to get along with each other."

The ideas that Jimi did have about Vietnam were wildly out of step with the antiwar movement. Eric Burdon recalls being with Jimi in Brook Street on Sunday, July 22, 1968, when a protest march against the war was shut out of Grosvenor Square and vented its anger against the Hilton Hotel in nearby Park Lane. Jimi defended the war like the former paratrooper he was: "Listen man, when the Red Chinese come screaming down over the borders of Laos, Cambodia and North Vietnam, and take over the whole of the Far East of Asia, you'll understand why the US is trying so hard in Vietnam."

chapter 16

haunting melodies

handel's ghost

Shortly after moving into Brook Street, Jimi discovered that he was not the first musician to live in the house. Over two hundred years before, it had been the home of George Frederick Handel.

Handel had come to London at the same age as Jimi had, though their backgrounds were very different. Handel had been born into an aspiring middle-class family in the German state of Saxony. His father was a surgeon who had hoped that his younger son would become a lawyer. Handel had had to keep his passion for music secret, studying by night on a clavier he kept hidden in the loft of the family home. When Handel's talent became recognized outside the family, his father gave in and Handel began a career in church music, as an assistant organist. The son compromised with his father too, and enrolled at the university to study law.

In the early eighteenth century, London was becoming an important musical city. With much of Europe at war, many musicians from across the Continent had taken refuge in England's capital city. Handel came to London on a sabbatical from his employment as court musician to George, the Elector of Hanover—and heir to the joint crowns of England and Scotland. Almost as soon as Handel arrived he began moonlighting—accepting commissions for the English court, then under Queen Anne, as well as writing for the opera house and familiarizing himself with the distinct traditions of English church music. When in 1715 George came to London as king, he initially snubbed Handel, but the new monarch could not ignore the composer's genius for long, and the two were reconciled.

The connection with the past sparked Jimi's interest in baroque music, and his flat soon rang with the music of Bach and Handel while he waited for couriers to bring tapes from Olympic studios. Always susceptible to occult ideas, and his imagination highly stimulated by regular LSD use, Jimi managed to persuade himself that he had seen a man in eighteenth-century dress walk through his bedroom wall one evening.

The two musicians would have found much in common. Handel was known to be temperamental when performances went awry. As a young man he had fought a duel on the steps of an opera house with a truculent violin player. Offstage he had a genial disposition and was fond of jokes.

the words of the prophet

By another coincidence, among Jimi's and Frederick's best-known works are their settings of the words of the prophet Isaiah.

On his return from the United States, Jimi had brought with him an advance copy of Bob Dylan's new album, *John Wesley Harding*. By the middle of 1968 Dylan had not toured or recorded for two years. When he finally presented a new set of master tapes to CBS Records, the executives heard something very different to the sound of *Blonde on Blonde*, the double album around which Jimi had forged his friendship with Linda Keith.

The music on *John Wesley Harding* is spare folk blues, with Dylan's guitar and harmonica filled out with only bass and drums. The lyrics are imagist in style, but the images are not the surreal and psychotically suggestive poetry of *Blonde on Blonde*. *John Wesley Harding* evokes icons of a mythical American landscape: outlaws, immigrants, hoboes, preachers, and whores. It is the work of a young artist (he was still only twenty-seven) brimming with self-confidence in his own judgment. After the unashamed sermonizing of "The Ballad of Frankie Lee and Judas Priest," the album closes with two straight country songs, a deeply unfashionable genre at the time.

Jimi's Harlem friends had dismissed Bob Dylan as a "cracker"— a very insulting word for a hillbilly. It was beginning to look as if they were right, to the dismay of the radical left, which had thought of Dylan as their spokesman, and to the alarm of CBS Records, which thought they had invested in an Elvis Presley with a high school diploma and a few comparative lit college credits.

With some foresight, CBS decided that if Jimi covered a song from *John Wesley Harding* it might pave the way to acceptance among rock fans of Dylan's apparently perverse change of direction. It was arranged that Jimi should have an advance copy, and he duly took the hint. When he arrived back in London he had already made up his mind to cover the ballad "I Dreamed I Saw St. Augustine."

When Kathy heard the record she thought differently. The song, she felt, was far too personal to Dylan. "All Along the Watchtower" seemed to her a better choice for Jimi.

Few would disagree with her now. Jimi's treatment of the song is inspired: a dramatic sound picture that picks up on the apocalyptic lyrics and presents them without melodrama or bathos. The words, as in many of Dylan's songs, are infused with biblical references; in this case the imagery comes from the Book of Isaiah. Jimi begins where Dylan's understated presentation finishes. The last lines of the song are "the wind began to howl." The wind is already rising in the opening bars of Jimi's cover, and the essence of rock and roll—a rising crescendo that never reaches a climax—is perfect for creating the suspenseful atmosphere of a cataclysmic prophecy about to be fulfilled.

Jimi drove the musicians who worked on "Watchtower" hard, insisting on take after take until they arrived at the sound he heard in his head. Kathy thought Jimi exhausted far too much studio time in pursuit of sounds that floated across his mind during acid trips but had little meaning to most listeners.

There is a strong tradition of mimetic sounds in African American music. Jimi himself turns in a good train impression in "Can You See Me?" on *Are You Experienced?* "All Along the Watchtower" conjures not only a tempest, but subtly, with the acoustic guitar, the rhythms of the horsemen already on their way to deliver their portentous message.

bare naked ladies

Kathy's gate-keeping could not stop Jimi from rolling home with friends and hangers-on. Carl Niekirk, who had a photography studio on the floor beneath the flat, recalls that he often answered the door to a keyless Jimi, and found him accompanied by famous faces. Niekirk recalls seeing George Harrison arrive on one occasion. Graham Nash was another visitor.

The same gregarious crowd followed Jimi to Olympic Studios, where *Electric Ladyland* was completed. Recording had begun earlier in the year at the Record Plant in New York City, which, apart from excellent engineering offered the novelty of twelve-track recording. As Jimi devoted more time to experimenting with the possibilities of the new technology, Mitch and Noel were pushed a little further into the background, and the long hiatuses in recording allowed the studio to fill up with hangers-on.

The London sessions for *Electric Ladyland* were equally crowded. The end of the long blues number "Voodoo Child" opens the microphone to the background noise in the studio, and above the hubbub of conversation a woman with an upper-class but piercing English accent is heard to inquire, "Is the bar still open?" The Rolling

Stones were at work on *Beggars' Banquet* at Olympic, and Brian Jones brought his sitar to one session for *Electric Ladyland*. Jimi experimented with the instrument, but quickly became frustrated with it.

Jimi's lyric writing remained a private activity. He wrote "1983 A Merman I Should Turn to Be" lying on the bed in Brook Street with Kathy beside him. When he read the words to her, including the line about going beneath the sea with his love Catherina, Kathy replied that she had no intention of living beneath the sea under any circumstances.

There was pressure for new material. The nine-month gap since the release of *Axis* seemed a long one by the standards of the time. Kit Lambert assembled and released a "best of" album as a potboiler. Jimi was also under pressure from Mike Jefferies to return to the United States, to begin the multicity tours that were to generate a small fortune. This was the pressure that prevailed, and Jimi, Noel, and Mitch flew to New York on July 27.

Electric Ladyland was released in London in November while Jimi was on the road. Jimi had had a very clear idea for the cover artwork and had sent rough sketches of his proposed layout. Kit Lambert took no notice of Jimi's ideas. He put the cover art into the hands of David King, the art editor of the *Sunday Times Colour Magazine*. He commissioned the photographer David Montgomery to photograph a studio of naked women, recumbent like odalisques in an Ingres harem. The women in the photograph were not professional models. They were assembled from the passersby outside Montgomery's Chelsea studio. The cornucopia of voluptuous female flesh, apparently as unretouched as it is unadorned, still has a powerful visceral impact in the age of instantly downloadable pornography. The women stare back at the viewer with a self-confidence that conveys as much threat as erotic promise. In Britain the LP was sold in a plain brown wrapper. There was no question of using it for the U.S. release, for fear it would offend traditional puritan sensitivities. No doubt it would have offended the nascent feminist movement too, but with the barricades barely dismantled on the Parisian boulevards the disappointments of the revolutionaries had yet to harden into the grievances of political correctness, and nobody on either side of the Atlantic considered the possibility that women might have an opinion about anything.

Jimi discovered what Kit had done only when he returned to London in January 1969, by which time all he could do was shrug the cover off.

chapter 17

the girl i left behind me

When Jimi, Noel, and Mitch returned to London in January 1969, they had decided that it was time to bring the Experience to an end. The band was Chas's creation and he was no longer involved. Noel and Mitch were recruits rather than members, and Noel was already involved with his own band, Fat Mattress.

Jimi had always preferred the idea of a larger ensemble that would play looser and more improvised sets. The more he fronted the Experience, the more he felt the need to jam, and the less opportunity he had to do so. The U.S. tour schedules had been frantic and intense, sometimes so intense as to cover thirty cities in as many days. In London Jimi had the **(32) Flamingo Club**, 33 Wardour Street, an afternoon club for musicians in Soho, where he could jam before he went to work, and the Speakeasy, where he could jam into the small hours.

Another influence on Jimi, Noel, and Mitch's decision to separate was that Cream had split up. The Experience had exceeded everyone's expectations, but had begun as a Cream imitation. It seemed to them pointless to continue as an imitation now that the original was no more.

On January 4, 1969, the Experience were guest stars on the *Happening for Lulu* show on BBC Television. Lulu, the show's presenter, was only twenty years old but had an extraordinary range of experience. Born Marie Lawrie in Lennoxtown, Scotland, in November 1948, she had been barely more than a child with an unusually strong voice when she had had her first British hit, "Shout," in her early teens. She had gone on to have hits in Europe (some recorded in German), and then appeared in the 1967 film *To Sir with Love*, playing a teenager, as she still was. She recorded the film's theme song, which became an international hit.

She had more than enough personality to present her own show, which aired early on Saturday evenings.

Jimi and the Experience performed "Voodoo Child (Slight Return)" and then Lulu announced that they would play their first hit, "Hey Joe," which, in the best tradition of TV presenters, "she loved." They began "Hey Joe," but after a lengthy intro, Jimi broke off and, with all good humor, told the studio audience that he was tired of "this shit" and would instead play a tribute to Cream. He then launched into "Sunshine of Your Love" (which Jack Bruce had written as a tribute to Jimi). When he finished, to polite applause, Jimi announced that they had been taken off the air because he had disrupted a tightly scheduled live show. The problem was that they hadn't been. The BBC was not a network and could not switch whatever it was broadcasting at short notice. It was a few minutes of chaos for the studio production team, who could not allow the show to overrun, and the BBC was not pleased. (By chance, a recording of the show survives and is often posted on YouTube.)

A month's tour of Scandinavia and Germany followed, and it was during this that Jimi very possibly had a brief fling with an ice skater named Monika Dannemann. If it took place it was a very fateful encounter. Jimi flew to New York to collect a *Billboard* award and returned quickly to London to prepare for two shows at the Royal Albert Hall a week apart. The venue was significant because it was where Cream had held their farewell concerts the previous November. Jimi, Noel, and Mitch thought of these gigs as the Experience's farewell performances in London. There was no formal announcement or any expectation of this news among the audiences. Many close to the band considered the performances, on February 18 and 24, half-hearted. During a solo of "Sunshine of Your Love," Jimi weaved in a few bars of "Strangers in the Night," just as on *Happening for Lulu* he had begun to pick out the riff from the Beatles' "Day Tripper" in his solo for "Voodoo Child." He was, in a way, jamming with himself.

Chas came to the first of the Albert Hall concerts and was unimpressed. If he had still been in charge, he would say later, he would have sacked Noel and Mitch the following day. Between the two concerts, all four of them met up to discuss the future, such as it was. Chas made it plain that if he was to have anything more to do with the Experience it would only be without Mike Jeffries. He gave Jimi, Noel, and Mitch a Mike-or-me ultimatum. Noel came away from the meeting with the impression that he, Jimi, and Mitch had all agreed that they would return to Chas, and was surprised over the following weeks that Mike was still very much in their lives.

Jimi's visions of his future were vague and sometimes grandiose. He sometimes foresaw himself presiding over a commune-cum-academy for musicians. At other times he considered putting his career to one side and going to college to study music. In practical terms Jimi's future, with or without the Experience, depended on Mike, and Mike's plans were very much wrapped around Jimi. Mike was eager to go into a business partnership with Jimi, and plans were evolving for a nightclub-cum-recording studio in New York City. This odd combination reflected the fact that nightclubs were the business Mike knew and a recording studio was what Jimi wanted. For the immediate future what counted was that plans for the project, which would be called Electric Lady whether it was a club or a studio or both, bound Jimi into a U.S. touring schedule that would be required to finance the project. Jimi hated to say the word "no" to anybody. Pressed by Chas to choose between him and Mike, Jimi would naturally choose whoever was in the room at the time. Noel and Mitch's opinions were irrelevant.

Jimi understood his position very well. In March he was interviewed by the *Melody Maker* and told the journalist Bob Dawbarn: "That's the trouble with this business. People see a fast buck and have you up there being a slave to the public. They keep you at it until you're exhausted and so is the public, then they move off to other things. That's why groups break up, they just get worn out. Musicians want to pull away after a time, or they get lost in the whirlpool." With an unhappy prescience he went on: "It's funny the way most people love the dead. Once you are dead you are made for life. You have to die before they think you are worth anything."

Jimi would be dead in eighteen months.

The pace of Jimi's life slowed briefly in the early spring of 1969, and he spent much time in Brook Street with Kathy, sometimes doing little more than watching television.

In early April Jimi, Noel, and Mitch flew back to the United States for their last tour together. Noel left when the tour ended at the end of June. Mitch joined Jimi at a farmhouse in upstate New York for what was part vacation and partly an experiment with Jimi's ideal for a musical commune. It was from there that Jimi arrived belatedly to close the Woodstock Festival, embellishing his reputation in the process.

For once, Kathy also attracted some media attention. The glossy magazine *Queen* ran a feature on rock stars' girlfriends and interviewed and photographed her. The feature was tied to the newly published novel *Groupie* by Jenny Fabian and Johnny Byrne.

Kathy was not a groupie; she was a hanger-out with musicians but not a hanger-on. The life of a groupie had no appeal to her, and when she was asked to live it, it marked the beginning of the end of her relationship with Jimi. He had flown to America to resume touring at the beginning of April, but it was not until September that Kathy flew out to join him in New York. She was appalled by what she found there. She hated the cocaine use that was widespread among Jimi's New York circle, and she feared the criminals who supplied it. And while some of her London friends happily adapted to the luxuries of hotel life, she hated that too. When she was not frightened, she was lonely and bored, and she soon flew home to London, never to return.

London moved on in Jimi's absence. The Beatles remained highly newsworthy, but interest was now focused on persistent rumors that they were on verge of splitting up. Yoko Ono had emerged from the avant-garde into the public eye that viewed her, unjustly, as an exotic vampirella who had sunk her fangs into a loveable mop-top and turned him peculiar. She had been a skillful self-publicist before she met John Lennon. When she turned the press harassment that surrounded her marriage to Lennon into conceptual art, journalists seized the photo opportunities greedily, and then, with cheerful hypocrisy, accused her of leeching off her husband's fame to enhance her artistic reputation. The public, disappointed that the cheekiest Beatle had lost his sense of humor, sided with the press.

Chas was beginning to work with a new act, a band from the Midlands called Ambrose Slade. Eventually he was to shorten their name to Slade and turn them into a very successful pop group, and their Christmas single, "Merry Xmas Everyone," a number one in 1973, is still heard in British stores throughout December as part of the seasonal background. Chas first tried to emulate Kit Lambert's strategy of associating the Who with the Mod movement by trying to associate Ambrose Slade with Skinheads. The Skinhead movement was largely made up of working-class boys who—eager to distance themselves from hippies—wore steel-capped boots, button-down shirts, pressed Levis, and close-cropped hair. They quickly earned a reputation for violence and racism.

And things moved on for Kathy when, in late 1969, she fell in love with another man and agreed to his proposal of marriage.

Jimi assumed that she was waiting in London for him, and went on assuming that until January of 1970, when he received a letter from her telling him that she was getting married and vacating their flat. It was far from welcome news at a point when Jimi was feeling frustrated with life on the road. He flew across the Atlantic to meet her at the beginning of February. Kathy was moved because it was the first time since he had become famous that she had ever known him to travel anywhere without his entourage. She was not moved enough to change her mind, however. Jimi stayed for a week in the Cumberland Hotel at Marble Arch, and by the time he returned to New York Kathy felt that he had accepted that their relationship, while not over, was now a friendship.

For over three years, home for Jimi had been wherever Kathy was, although he had spent less and less time there. Now he was homeless.

Not that Jimi would have had much use for a home during the closing months of his life. The summer of 1970 was spent on tour in the United States. It was a way of life he came to increasingly resent, yet had no escape from. The debts incurred for the Electric Lady project kept him bound to an exhausting schedule. The mountainous rages he had exhibited at the frustrations of broken equipment became ineffectual tantrums against the cold logic of the balance sheet, which he was complicit with. So he began to turn his hostility on the audiences, who still called for "Fire" and "Purple Haze." Whereas once he had made his guitar intone "thank you," now it said "fuck you."

Some respite came with another Mike Jefferies project, the ill-conceived, or rather barely conceived, *Rainbow Bridge*, a rambling psychedelic movie that was intended to change the consciousness of the entire world. Jimi's role in it was small, but it did allow him to kill several weeks in a hotel in Hawaii, waiting to film his contribution. The only bankable performer in the project, he was at the same time the project's banker because once more the money was raised against Jimi's future earnings.

chapter 18

tomorrow or the end of time

the island time forgot

Jimi's last journey across the Atlantic was to play at the Isle of Wight Festival.

The Isle of Wight seemed an incongruous location for a pop festival. The island, off the south coast of England, had been untouched by the excitements of the 1960s. Nor had the 1950s or even the war years of the 1940s made much of an impact on the island's way of life: seaside resorts on the coast and farming inland. In the event, however, the first great Isle of Wight Festival of 1969 had been a friendly affair on both sides. The islanders and the more conventional holidaymakers enjoyed the novelty of the picturesque invasion. They had seen newspaper stories about boys who wore their hair like girls, and youngsters who preferred to go barefoot even if they could afford shoes, but they had never seen these people, and tens of thousands of them had turned up all at once. As for festival-goers, what Tolkien-reading hippy could fail to love an island where the major art form is the garden gnome?

The first festival had been held in 1968, as a very small affair, but the second, held in August 1969, had pulled off a great coup by persuading Bob Dylan to top the bill. The organizers of the now legendary Woodstock Festival of 1969 chose Woodstock as the venue because it was the home of Bob Dylan, and they hoped—forlornly, as it turned out—that the event would lure the Jester from the sidelines to claim the thorny crown of the Woodstock generation. The Isle of Wight prevailed where Woodstock had failed. At the end of August 1969 Dylan brought his family to stay in a farmhouse outside the yachting resort of Bembridge, and he played a short set to a crowd of 200,000 on Wootoon Down, his first public paid appearance in four years and almost his last for another four.

To rub Woodstock's nose even deeper into the mud, the Isle of Wight booked Jimi, the hero of Woodstock, to play at the 1970 Isle of Wight Festival.

Jimi arrived in London directly from the party on August 26 for the opening night of the ill-considered Electric Lady Studios in New York City. The young Patti Smith had attempted to gatecrash the party but lost her nerve. "I was too shy to go in, so I sat on the steps," she told the journalist Ed Vulliamy in an interview in 2005. "And out came Hendrix; he asked me what I was doing and he said, 'Hey, I'm kind of shy too.' So we sat on the steps and he talked about what he was going to do when he got back from London; how he was going to create a new language of rock 'n' roll; I was so excited. And then he was gone. He never came back."

tear down the fences

Ed Vulliamy was at the 1970 Isle of Wight Festival as a six-teen-year-old schoolboy. The mood he found there had little do with Woodstock, and was attuned to his own mind. "I was rather a severe young man, quite political," he recalls now. "These were the days when the left was quite heavy, in the slipstream of May 1968 and the

Paris riots. I wasn't interested in hippies but I found Yippies quite interesting. So I was quite gratified when some French anarchists decide to tear down the fences because they didn't think there should be tickets."

Ed Vulliamy was at the front of the crowd when Jimi came on stage in a flowing orange costume:

> I couldn't tell you if he played for an hour, two hours, or three hours. It seemed like a goddamn eternity. It was incredibly loud, overwhelming. It is a shame that contemporary language has now destroyed the word "awesome."
>
> I remember it finishing. I remember my ears hurting. I was sitting down with some people I'd met. I don't think any of us said very much. It took a long time to de-rig.
>
> I don't remember any specific song, just this barrage. This may sound pretentious but I had begun to like Wagner then and it was like Wagner—dangerous. It plays to a place inside you, not necessarily a place you want to go.

a future that didn't exist

Just before Jimi set off for the Isle of Wight, an interview session had been arranged at the Londonderry Hotel. Norman Joplin was then editor of the magazine *Music Now,* and was notified of the opportunity at the last minute. There were no other journalists in the office, so he went and did the interview himself.

"Jimi must have been talking for hours to dozens of reporters and posing for photographers," he recalls now,

> but when my turn came for the interview—I was last—he was relaxed, energetic, laughing, seeming like he was having a good time. When I suggested

he might be stressed out with all the interviews, he was adamant he was fine with it all: "But a few months ago, no way," he said. "You know, if I even thought anyone was coming into the room, I'd go and hide in the wardrobe. Now I'm OK again."

He seemed extremely together; wasn't on drugs (and there was no residual drugginess about him), he was thoughtful, he was very intelligent, and he was warm. But most strikingly he was also physically very attractive, more so than in photographs or on film.

Joplin asked Jimi about the Electric Lady Studios. "It's a very relaxing studio and it doesn't have that studio atmosphere," Jimi said. "There are lots of cushions and pillows and soft lights. You can have any kind of light combination you want. I'm into this combination of music and color—it's an extra area of awareness. I'm thinking about a film using those techniques." Meanwhile, Jimi told Joplin, there would be a new LP in October and a double album after that.

In fact the immediate future was not as rosy as Jimi made out. The new album was still boxes and boxes of tapes of chaotic jam sessions that Eddie Kramer was attempting to mix into shape back in New York.

The splendors of Electric Lady remained unpaid for, and Jimi was heavily in debt. Jimi was not a free man. The only means of servicing, let alone paying, his debts was touring. "I wanted to come back [to England]," Jimi told Joplin that evening, "but the people said well you're playing in Boston on so and so day and all that." Jimi did not mention the flying visit he had made to London six months earlier to try to recover Kathy's heart.

Touring was a constraint not only on his time but also on his artistic development. Jimi's U.S. appearances were heralded on the new FM radio networks with advertisements based around "Purple Haze." Jimi had tried to leave the Experience behind at the Royal Albert Hall eighteen months before, but it was the Experience that the public wanted to see.

"When it was the Experience there was more room for ego-tripping you know?" he told Joplin. "All I had to blast off stage were a drummer and a bass! But now I want to step back and let other things come forward. This is the idea of my getting a band together, a big band to develop new ideas. I don't know what my music will be like, I don't know if I'm playing differently now."

To add to these complications Jimi had been followed over the Atlantic by a law suit. In 1965, while still a sideman and session man, Jimi had signed a loose and unadvised contract with a New York record producer called Ed Chalpin. When in early 1967 Mike Jeffries had sent an emissary to track down and buy out any contract Jimi might have signed, the arrangement with Chalpin had slipped Jimi's mind.

Chalpin was in no mood to be bought off. His pride was wounded; he considered Jimi his discovery, stolen from him by Frank Sinatra's label Warner Brothers. Chalpin saw himself as a black David oppressed by the Goliath of white big business. By 1970 a legal settlement had been arrived at between Warner Brothers and Chalpin, but a still aggrieved Chalpin had begun a legal action in the High Court in London against Polydor, the distributor for Track Records.

Behind the bold face Jimi presented to the press, the strain of his many problems gnawed away at him, and his attempts to escape them through reckless living undermined his health and mental stability further. On the night of his press interviews, Kathy got a call from a friend who was at the Londonderry Hotel in Jimi's suite. She and another girl had been with Jimi in his bedroom when he had turned on them and pushed them out. Now they were naked and stranded. Kathy went to the Londonderry and talked her way into his bedroom. It was a warm sunny evening but the heating was on, and as Kathy gathered up the girls' clothes, Jimi was rolled up tight in his bed, silent and shivering.

a bad trip

Whatever Jimi's plans for the future, he had brought a three-piece band with him to play the Isle of Wight and the short tour of Scandinavia and Northern Europe that was to take place immediately afterward. Mitch Mitchell was on the drums and Noel's role was taken by Billy Cox, Jimi's best friend from the army.

Cox was a shy man and the tour was his first trip out of the United States. He felt out of his depth as a musician and was afraid that he would let Jimi down. Both Jimi and Mitch shared a "blast 'em off the stage" attitude and gave little leeway to each other or Billy. In Sweden somebody spiked Billy's drink with LSD. He had no experience of acid and was plunged into paranoid delusions over a plot to kill him and Jimi.

In Copenhagen Jimi had an attack of nervous exhaustion, which caused him to cut the show short. It is possible that somebody had slipped him LSD backstage.

The tour moved on to another festival, at Freham Island in Germany. The festival site had been taken over by warring gangs of outlaw motorcyclists. The band had to take shelter in a trailer with a shooting war going on outside. By the time the tour reached Amsterdam it was plain that it would have to be abandoned and that Billy, who was in a state of complete mental breakdown, would have to be sent home.

moon turn the tides

Back in London, Jimi paid a visit to Chas. He and Lotta were married now, and Jimi met their infant son for the first time. There was a game of *Risk*, for old time's sake, then some talk of the future when Jimi asked Chas if we would take over as producer of the album due in October. It was an acknowledgement on Jimi's part that his best studio work had been accomplished under Chas's direction.

Chas did agree that if Jimi brought the tapes and Eddie Kramer over from New York, he would book studio time at Olympic. When Jimi called New York, Eddie Kramer misunderstood, and thought he was on the end of peremptory and prima donna-ish summons to London, a futile expedition when Jimi was due back in New York within a week, so he ignored the request.

On the night of Tuesday, September 15, Jimi turned up at Ronnie Scott's, where Eric Burdon had a week's residency to launch his new band, War. Jimi wanted to jam but was clearly in no condition to play. He cut a strange, gothic figure in a black cape and broad-brimmed hat, and he was accompanied by a tall and forbiddingly silent blonde in heavy make-up. His friend Sharon Lawrence, a UPI agency journalist, was appalled at how distant he seemed. Although their paths had crossed days ago in Copenhagen, he did not recognize her at first. The following night, Wednesday, Jimi returned to Ronnie Scott's and played brilliantly. Nevertheless, Sharron Lawrence was still worried enough to phone him at the Cumberland Hotel in Marble Arch the following morning. Jimi recited a litany of his troubles to her. The law suit made him miserable, and some of his entourage from New York had arrived and begun making demands on him. Lawrence promised she would phone later.

That afternoon Mitch had a phone call from Jimi. Sly Stone was due to fly into Heathrow that evening, and Jimi suggested to Mitch that the three of them meet up at the Speakeasy that night. Mitch waited for the phone call that would confirm this arrangement, but it never came.

Instead, Jimi struck up a friendship with a pair of complete strangers in Park Lane and went to a party at their house. He was collected by two women, a blonde and a black woman, in the early hours of September 18. His hosts heard a quarrel outside on the pavement. These two women were the last to see Jimi alive.

On the sunny afternoon of Friday, September 18, Ed Vulliamy was on his way home to Holland Park from his school in Hampstead. The boards for London's evening newspapers were out and carried the news that Jimi Hendrix had been found dead. For the first time in his life Ed bought an evening paper. On his way home he read that Jimi had been found dead at the **(33) Samarkand Hotel,** 21-22 Lansdowne Crescent, which was almost directly at the end of the street where Ed lived. Locally, the Samarkand had an exotic reputation. It did not advertise itself as a hotel at all—its only sign was an esoteric stained-glass Tibetan symbol—but it was known as a haunt of visiting American rock stars.

When he got home, Ed changed out of his school uniform, and went, dressed all in white on a personal pilgrimage. Lansdowne Crescent is a curved street of nineteenth-century houses with white stucco fronts and imposing porticoes. It leads nowhere, and when Ed arrived that evening it was deserted. He had some chalk with him and he drew a personal memorial to Jimi on the pavement outside the Samarkand. Among the words he wrote were "Moon Turn the Tides Gently, Gently Away," a tune from *Electric Ladyland* that Ed personally felt expressed the shift from life to death. Then he crossed the street and kept vigil alone. Dusk fell and then darkness, and a janitor came up from the basement of the Samarkand with a mop and bucket and washed the chalk marks away.

For all anybody knew at the time, all the traces of Jimi Hendrix would be washed away once the sensation of his death died down. Along Fleet Street, which was then the heart of London's newspaper industry, journalists reached for their cuttings files to find out the "who?" as much as the "what?" and the "why?" British journalists do not regard themselves as history's stenographers, as many U.S. journalists do, but as her handmaids, always ready to put beauty before truth. By Sunday, the day traditionally reserved for the most scandalous journalism, one such enterprising soul had typed an account of Jimi's supposed last phone call to his manager, livened up with the sort of hip slang found in public information films about drug abuse.

Those who knew Jimi, most of whom learned of his death through news reports, felt shock more than grief, and sadness for times lost. None of them expected him to be turned into a god.

chapter 19

sad stories of the death of kings

in the wink of an eye

Death made Jimi into something he had never been before: a celebrity. In life he had been a charismatic man; in death he acquired the far feebler and insubstantial luster of glamour.

Celebrities are figures of fantasy, and dead people are easier to fantasize about because they will not change or disappoint us by becoming fundamentalist Christians or selling real estate. (Kathy Etchingham became a very successful realtor.) And they will not age, which makes the process of apotheosis—becoming a god—all the more convincing.

Jimi's memory deserves better than this. Because of the association of death with celebrity, the death of someone on the brink of celebrity is referred to with a cynical irony as a career move. But death did Jimi's reputation as a musician no favors. Apart, of course, from denying him the chance to mature musically, death robbed him of any chance to take control of and edit his back catalogue and to prevent the release of a torrent of material, official and unofficial, that poured out to fill the void. Even as his life closed he was unhappy with the way pirated tapes and contractual obligations were bringing substandard work into circulation. In 1970 the mass media took far less interest in rock stars than it does now. Jimi had topped polls in the music press for three years, and would continue to do so well into the 1970s. When he died, however, he was still unknown to the vast majority of people, who took no interest in progressive rock. None of the people who became officially involved with his death—the emergency services, the doctors, and the coroner—had ever heard of him. It was his death that brought the mass media to his door, and when it arrived, because he was relatively unknown, he was easy to caricature as a self-destructive hedonist.

the mystery of monika

Central to the events of Jimi's death was Monika Dannemann, a twenty-six-year-old from Dusseldorf in West Germany. In her youth she had enjoyed modest success as a competitive ice skater until an injury ended her career. The death of Jimi became the central event of Monika Dannemann's life, until she committed suicide in 1996, when she gassed herself with a hosepipe attached to the exhaust pipe of her car in the garage of her home in rural Sussex in the south of England.

As the woman there at the time, the title of Jimi's widow was thrust upon Monika and she hung on to it tenaciously. Various parties at various times supported her claim for their own ends.

Monika was capable of being calculating. As early as September 19, 1970—the day after he died—she began to use conversations about Jimi's death and Jimi in general to fish for information that she would later recycle as her own testimony. Yet she often regurgitated information regardless of whether it was in her interest to do so or not. Possibly over the years she came to believe that the figment of her imagination she named Jimi Hendrix had asked her to marry him. Wherever one draws the line between the fantasist and the liar, nothing she ever said can be taken as reliable.

Monika's involvement with Jimi's life, as opposed to his death, added up to less than a week. In the third week of September 1970 Monika approached Alvinia Hedges, Eric Burdon's girlfriend, in the Speakeasy. Monika claimed that she and Alvinia had worked together two summers previously. Alvinia's own memory required some prompting before she recalled that they had. Then Monika told Alvinia of her passion for Jimi. She had met him a couple of years ago; he had taken her virginity, and she was deeply in love with him. Touched by this forlorn woman, Alvinia phoned Jimi and asked him to come to the Speakeasy.

Monika was Jimi's companion for the last few days of his life—the woman Sharon Lawrence saw with Jimi at Ronnie Scott's and the woman who collected Jimi from a party in the early hours of Friday, September 18. On this occasion she appears to have been accompanied by Devon Wilson, who Jimi had known first in his Harlem days and had become part of his New York entourage. Party guests heard raised voices in the street. Where and when Devon left Jimi and Monika that night remains a mystery. Jimi and Monika went back to the Samarkand Hotel.

At some time between 6 a.m. and 6:30 a.m. Monika phoned Alvinia in Eric Burdon's hotel room. She told Alvinia that Jimi was ill, and asked her if she knew the telephone number of Jimi's doctor. In 1970 Britain was in the second year of an experiment with double summer time (known to Americans as daylight savings time), and so, although it was 6 a.m., the streets were still dark. It felt as if it was the middle of the night. If Monika felt she had had time to search through Jimi's papers for a doctor's number, as she said she had, this could hardly be a pressing emergency. Alvinia, with Eric at her elbow, suggested that Monika call an ambulance.

Around 11 a.m. Monika phoned Alvinia and Eric again. Already worried that he should have done more, Eric became insistent that an ambulance be called and set off to the Samarkand with Alvinia. The emergency call for an ambulance was logged at 11:18 a.m.

nothing but death

The two-man ambulance crew found the door of the hotel room open and Jimi lying on the bed, covered in vomit, "vomit of all colours, black and brown, all over him and all over the pillow," one of the ambulance crew told Kathy Etchingham more than twenty years later. Jimi appeared lifeless; an aspirator was fetched from the ambulance, but he could not be revived. The ambulance crew called for the police over the radio, and two beat officers arrived.

It is here that corners were cut. The beat officers should have called in a detective. Rather than face a day of filling in forms and tracing next of kin, however, the police constables persuaded the ambulance crew to take Jimi's body to the hospital and have him admitted as an emergency. When the ambulance arrived at the hospital, Jimi was pronounced dead by the doctor on duty and sent straight to the mortuary.

with rainy eyes

Strong emotion can color memory, and for many years afterward Eric Burdon believed that he had seen Jimi dead on the bed. He arrived at the Samarkand with Alvinia at around 11:45 a.m., when the ambulance had already left. Monika emerged from somewhere, and the young women embraced each other and wailed. Eric wandered around and found a long poem in Jimi's handwriting beside the bed. Gerry Stickells, the Experience's first roadie, was sent for, to take Jimi's guitars into safekeeping and to remove any drugs in case there was to be a police search. When asked what she had done between her first call to Alvinia and Eric and her second, all Monika found to say is that she had gone out to buy cigarettes. It was the only clear statement she was ever to make about the events of September 18, 1970.

some kind of way out of here

The day after Jimi died, Sharron Lawrence was introduced to Monika by Eric Burdon at his hotel. She asked Monika what drugs Jimi had taken and was told Vesperax.

Vesperax is a secobarbitol. Secobarbitols are efficient painkillers but in the 1960s they were frequently prescribed for insomnia, and even for anxiety. They are potentially lethal; before they were withdrawn in the late 1980s, they had become the drug of choice in medically assisted suicides.

Monika was prescribed Vesperax for the pain she still suffered from the accident that had ended her skating career. She had four packs of ten pills with her in the Smarakand. It is not clear whether Monika recommended the pills as something that would help Jimi sleep, or whether he had found them himself in the bathroom. Monika found a sachet from one pack on the bathroom floor, with only one of the pills left in it. This implied that Jimi had taken nine Vesperax.

The number made an impression on Lawrence. Jimi had strong faith in numerolgy, or number divination, and believed that the number nine held personal significance for him. September is the ninth month of the year, and the eighteenth is a nine day.

On the same occasion, Eric Burdon showed Sharon Lawrence the writing he had found beside Jimi's bed, a poem that closed with the ominous lines, "In the wink of an eye/life is hello and goodbye." Lawrence thought it significant that the writing had been found at all. She knew Jimi well enough to know that he made a point of tidying his writing away in a burgundy folder when he was finished with it. He had told her he did this to stop his work from being pilfered by souvenir hunters. From the symbolism of the number of pills, and the fact that his last poem had been left where it would be found, Lawrence concluded that Jimi had meant to end his life.

open verdict

The inquest into Jimi's death opened at **(34) Westminster Coroner's Court**, 65 Horseferry Road, a squat little building a few hundred yards from Westminster Abbey, on Tuesday, September 24, the day after an autopsy had been performed. The inquest was immediately adjourned to the following Monday, September 28, to allow the pathologist time to complete tests.

When the inquest reopened, the coroner, Dr. Gavin Thurston, was evidently determined to protect Jimi's reputation. Monika Dannemann was the main witness. She described herself as a friend (not, as yet, the fiancée she would later claim to have been), and said she had known Jimi since January 1969 (she may have met him them). She told the court that she had collected Jimi from a party at 3 a.m., and had taken a sleeping pill before going to bed. She said that she had woken up at around 10:30 a.m. and found Jimi sleeping peacefully. She said that she then went out to buy a packet of cigarettes and that when she came back she found Jimi was ill and called an ambulance. The coroner asked Monika if Jimi had used hard drugs. Monika said that she thought he might have tried them in the past but was not involved with them. The coroner was satisfied with this answer.

The pathologist, Professor Donald Teare, gave the cause of Jimi's death as inhalation of vomit due to barbiturate poisoning. This meant that Jimi did not die because he vomited in his sleep, but vomited because he was already dying. It is a subtlety that is easy to miss.

As to Jimi's state of mind, the coroner made much of Gerry Stickell's testimony that Jimi was "a happy chap." Roadies are not renowned for their penetrating psychological skills, but it was a view many other people would have expressed.

English coroner's juries usually deliver the verdict as the coroner directs them to. This case was no exception, and the result was an "open verdict." The significance is that although Jimi's death could not be declared "accidental," it was not "misadventure" either, that is, careless or reckless behavior. He died of a drug overdose, but he did not die from substance abuse.

Sharron Lawrence, who was present, was appalled then, and is appalled now, that suicide was not considered. Until 1960 suicide and attempted suicide were criminal offenses in England. Attempted suicides were placed under arrest as soon as they regained consciousness. To spare the feelings of the family and friends of the deceased, English coroners will avoid delivering a verdict of "suicide" whenever they can, even if the deceased died of something patently suicidal such as jumping under a moving train. An open verdict is delivered in such cases, too, but in this instance Dr. Thurston appears to have been concerned to exonerate Jimi from being declared a drug addict.

Jimi's state of mind in the last days of his life was mysterious even to those who knew him well. Nobody can be sure how he came to take nine Vesperax (if it was in fact nine—four would have been enough to be fatal). Perhaps he was putting his life into the hands of cosmic forces as a test of whether he should live or die. Or perhaps he felt he needed some rest.

A distressed Monika Dannemann, escorted by Gerry Stickells, is driven away from Jimi's inquest.

afterword

if six were nine

"I would like to think that even without the foresight of Chas, Jimi would have made it ultimately, but there is always that doubt. So much of it was a matter of alchemy, timing, luck or whatever."
— *Mitch Mitchell*

There is a very human tendency to see success as inevitable, if not foreordained. We are all far readier to discount good luck as opposed to bad luck. Nobody would have thought Jimi's life a fortunate life until he met Chas. Is there any good reason to suppose it would have become a fortunate one if he never had?

Several of the musicians Jimi had gathered around him at the Cafe Wha? went on to better things. Randy California joined the much underrated Spirit. Jeff Baxter helped launch adult-oriented rock with Steely Dan and the Doobie Brothers. And Jimi might have made name for himself playing blues. The sharp-eared Roger Mayer had already noticed Jimi's guitar work on the only significant recording he made before he came to London, Don Covay's "Mercy Mercy." So it is certainly possible—albeit maybe not probable—that Jimi would have made a reputation of some kind for himself whatever had happened to him after 1966.

Jimi Hendrix was fortunate to find London. Almost as soon as his reputation emerged, it was said in jest that he represented a reverse British invasion, and that he had crossed the Atlantic to storm

Britain in the same way the Beatles and other British bands had stormed America. The joke ignored the fact that Jimi Hendrix was a British act, as Jimi himself said when asked by British journalists if he represented New York music.

In New York Jimi had found himself out of step with his contemporaries through his love of the blues and the contempt he felt for Motown. In London there was still an audience for the blues, and, more helpfully still for Jimi, an audience with an interest in guitar virtuosity due to the competitive rivalry of a talented generation of guitarists: Eric Clapton, Jeff Beck, Jimmy Page, Pete Townsend, and Brian Jones, among others.

Jimi's appeal was his virtuosity rather than his authenticity as a bluesman. London allowed him to sidestep some racial expectations that had limited him in his own country. When Chris Welch first saw Jimi perform, he was surprised to see an African American playing rock rather than what in Britain was known as soul music, but it was something that Welch and everybody else easily accepted.

Jimi also arrived at a time when London's recording studios were at their best. Technically they lagged behind American studios, but the technical limitations had created an innovative generation of recording engineers. British record labels still thought of themselves as largely in the business of recording and selling classical music. Their executives did not understand popular music, and did not want to, which gave record producers a free creative hand.

Left to himself, Jimi might never have become a front man at all, because he did not think much of his singing. The initial inspiration came from Chas, and it was Chas's contacts that smoothed his way into London. Kathy's contacts were helpful too; it was through her that he met Brian Jones and secured the interest of the Beatles.

Yet London was fortunate in finding Jimi Hendrix too. There was a hunger for experiment among London musicians, partly inspired by avant-garde jazz and partly inspired by a general desire to explore new possibilities. There were, however, no musicians capable of great originality. The skilled, such as Eric Clapton, were in awe of the bluesmen who had inspired them. The daring, such as Pink Floyd, were scarcely musicians at all. Jimi's knowledge of music theory was limited, but he was a highly skilled musician (his skill is still often underestimated: even when jamming he could repeat any phrase he had played or play it backwards if asked to). He was also a swift and eager learner who adapted and adopted new sounds very quickly. He had a great deal to say for himself musically, and had had very few opportunities to say it before he moved to London.

There was much in Jimi's life that could have caused a different man to feel bitterness, resentment, or grievance. Jimi drew on his experiences to bring greater emotional depth to his music. After Jimi was gone, many rock musicians attempted to emulate classical music by increasing the scale, the complexity, and the length of their performances. They failed, because what rock lacked in comparison with classical music was not complexity but feeling. While Jimi's songs are unlikely to become central to the classical repertoire, he is today admired by classical musicians such as the violinist Nigel Kennedy.

* * *

Had Jimi not died in 1970, what would he recognize in contemporary London? All the places where he lived still stand. The flat in Brook Street is now the offices of the Handel Trust, which are occasionally opened for short tours on weekends. The Speakeasy and the Scotch have long since closed, but the buildings that housed them remain. The site of UFO has been redeveloped. The interior of Olympic Studios have been rebuilt beyond recognition, De Lane Lea Studios have been demolished. The site of the tiny Regent Studios on Denmark Street is now a music shop, where passersby are welcome to drop in and take a quick look.

Jimi's ghost might be pleased to find that Jimi's life is commemorated in London. There is a blue commemorative plaque on the house in Brook Street, one of those plaques installed by the English

Heritage organization to mark the homes of distinguished former residents of England. The auditorium of the Central Polytechnic is now the Law School of the University of Westminster. Its glass doors are engraved with a memorial to Jimi's first London appearance. Ronnie Scott's, where Jimi made his last appearance on stage ever, is still open for business on Frith Street.

Jimi's unmistakeable image crops up in all kinds of unofficial sites, too. He remains a gift to visual artists, and I have seen his haunting face staring from the window of backstreet poster shops, on decorative mirrors, even as a limited-edition table lamp. No caption seems to be required to explain who he was; he remains emblematic of a time and a place, but free of nostalgia. As I write, there is a revived interest in progressive music, and just as I rediscovered Jimi as the father of Funk, there will be inquiring ears searching him out for the first time as the founder of that, in formats that were beyond imagining in the 1960s.

In a playful film clip in 1967, Mitch and Noel interview Jimi. "Is it true," he is asked, "that you play guitar with your tongue?" "No," Jimi replies, "I play the guitar with my ear." And it is by the ear he would have preferred to be remembered. And he will be.

notes

chapter 1

8: "Chas had made up ...": Charles Cross, *A Room Full of Mirrors* (London: Sceptre, 2005), 142–154.

15: "They were also ...": Harry Shapiro, *Alexis Korner: The Biography* (London: Bloomsbury, 1996), 81.

15: "It was a corny line ...": Kathy Etchingham, *Through Gypsy Eyes* (London: Victor Gollancz, 1998), 60.

chapter 2

19: "Jeffries had been ...": John McDermott with Eddie Kramer, *Jimi Hendrix: Setting The Record Straight* (London: Little Brown, 1993), 61–62.

23: "Kathy made several ...": Etchingham, *Through Gypsy Eyes,* 85, 68.

chapter 3

26: "Eric Clapton's reputation ...": Shapiro, *Alexis Korner*, 80–83 and 103–104.

27: "Baker had had no formal ...": Michael Schumacher, *Crossroads: The Life and Music of Eric Clapton* (London: Little, Brown, 1995), 69–72.

28: "Baker then insisted ...": Schumacher, *Crossroads,* 80.

chapter 4

35: "Actual Mods cared ...": Geoffrey Giuliano, *Behind Blue Eyes: A Life Of Pete Townshend* (London: Hodder & Stoughton, 1996), 53–55.

36: "In Britain's industrial ...": Geoffrey Pearson, *Hooligan: A History of Respectable Fears* (London: Macmillan, 1983), 92–101.

chapter 5

40: "It was not quite ...": Chris Welch, *Hendrix, A Biography* (London: Ocean Books, 1972), 9.

40: "Chris Welch was not ...": Giuliano, *Behind Blue Eyes*, 72.

41: "Jimi's claims may ...": Richard Maloof, *Jim Marshall: The Father of Loud* (London: Backbeat Books, 2004).

43: "Ringo had fitted ...": Etchingham, *Through Gypsy Eyes,* 85.

46: "I have been watching ...": Welch, *Hendrix*, 17.

chapter 6

49: "Even the orthodox usage ...": Sharron Lawrence, *Jimi Hendrix, the Magic, the Truth* (London: Sidgwick & Jackson, 2005), 62.

chapter 7

53: "Hendrix appears at ...": Lawrence, *Jimi Hendrix, the Magic, the Truth*, 71.

57: "The onstage Jimi...": Roger Mayer, interview with the author, at the Worcester Park pub, Park Terrace, Worcester Park, Surrey, September 20, 2005.

chapter 8

59: "Sometimes they found themselves ...": Lawrence, *Jimi Hendrix, the Magic, the Truth*, 72.

62: "For all his skills ...": Mayer, interview with the author.

65: "Kathy had no inclination ...": Etchingham, *Through Gypsy Eyes,* 89.

chapter 9

68: "Then things went more dramatically ...": *Melody Maker,* April 8, 1967, 1.

69: "Relationships were not ...": Mitch Mitchell with John Platt, *The Hendrix Experience* (London: Pyramid Books, 1990), 49.

69: "The hi-fi system was a bit ...": Etchingham, *Through Gypsy Eyes,* 99.

71: "Ambivalent as Jimi felt ...": Etchingham, *Through Gypsy Eyes,* 91.

72: "For three days ...": June Southworth, email to author, March 8, 2007.

72: "*Fabulous,* which devoted much space ...": *Fabulous 208,* June 26, 1967, 6.

73: "Southworth was charmed ...": Southworth, email to the author.

chapter 10

76: "The ancient music …": Michael Hollingshead, *The Man Who Turned on the World* (London: Blond & Briggs Ltd., 1973), chapter 6.

78: "LSD was initially …": George Melly, "Poster Power," *Observer Colour Supplement,* December 3, 1967, 13.

79: "An anonymous …": *Melody Maker,* May 20, 1967, 13.

80: "Naturally there were …": Melly, "Poster Power," 9.

80: "Drug taking for a time …": *Financial Times,* December 28, 1967.

82: "The LP …": *International Times,* no. 14, June 2, 1967, 12.

83: "We just used to chat …": Mayer, interview with the author.

chapter 11

86: "Arrived in Belgravia …": Joe Orton, *The Orton Diaries,* ed. John Lahr (London: Methuen, 1986), 73–74.

88: "One of Epstein's …": Noel Redding and Carol Appleby, *Are You Experienced?* (London: Fourth Estate, 1990), 52.

88: "It's still obviously …": Barry Miles, *Paul McCartney: Many Years from Now* (London: Secker & Warburg, 1997), 347.

89: "It was never a question …": Mayer, interview with the author.

chapter 12

93: "At the junction …": Joe Boyd, *White Bicycles: Making Music in the 1960s* (London: Serpent's Tail, 2006), 143–149.

93: "Mark Boyle, who ran …": http://www.boylefamily.co.uk/boyle/texts/journey2.html.

95: "Jimi was very interested …": Mayer, interview with the author.

chapter 13

97: "'*Axis Bold as Love,* that was the album for me, …": Mayer, interview with the author.

98: "Chas and Jimi quarreled …": Welch, *Hendrix*, 50.

99: "Olympic Studios now had …": Mayer, interview with the author.

chapter 14

102: "Extreme crowd behavior …": Nick Mason, *Inside Out: A Personal History of Pink Floyd* (London: Weidenfield & Nicolson, 2004), 96.

102: "Kathy had taken …": Etchingham, *Through Gypsy Eyes*, 99–100.

104: "It seemed to Noel …": Mayer, interview with the author.

105: "Underground London finished …": Redding and Carol Appleby, *Are You Experienced?*, 72.

chapter 15

108: "Kathy never found out …": Welch, *Hendrix*, 50.

110: "A lifelike rubber rat …": *Melody Maker*, March 4, 1969, 12.

112: "Tucked away …": Etchingham, *Through Gypsy Eyes*, 114–115.

112: "The ideas that …": Eric Burdon with J. Marshall Craig, *Don't Let Me Be Misunderstood* (New York: Thunder's Mouth Press, 2001).

chapter 16

116: "Kathy's gate-keeping …": *Independent on Sunday,* March 22, 2009.

chapter 17

121: "Chas came to the first …": McDermott with Kramer, *Jimi Hendrix: Setting The Record Straight*, 172.

chapter 18

126: "Jimi arrived…": "Some Gave a Song, Some Gave a Life," interview with Patti Smith, *Guardian,* June 3, 2005. http://www.guardian.co.uk/music/2005/jun/03/meltdownfestival2005.meltdownfestival.

126: "Ed Vulliamy was at …": Ed Vulliamy, interview with the author at his home, January 4, 2006.

127: "Jimi must have been talking ….": Norman Joplin, email to the author, November 8, 2005.

128: "Joplin asked Jimi …": *Music Now,* September 12, 1970.

129: "Behind the bold face …": Etchingham, *Through Gypsy Eyes,* 147.

131: "Chas did agree ...": McDermott with Kramer, *Jimi Hendrix: Setting The Record Straight*, 358.

131: "On the night ...": Lawrence, *Jimi Hendrix, the Magic, the Truth*, 215.

131: "That afternoon ...": Mitchell with Platt, *The Hendrix Experience*, 157–159.

131: "On the sunny afternoon ...": Vulliamy, interview with the author.

chapter 19

135: "Monika's involvement ...": David Henderson, *The Life of Jimi Hendrix: 'Scuse Me While I Kiss the Sky* (London: Omnibus, 1990), 278.

137: "On the same occasion ...": Lawrence, *Jimi Hendrix, the Magic, the Truth*, 219.

afterword

141: "I would like to think ...": Mitchell with Platt, *The Hendrix Experience*.

credits

about the author

William Saunders was born in London in 1958 and began his writing career in the underground magazines that sprang up around the punk movement at the end of the 1970s. One of his songs was played on the legendary John Peel show, and an early poem awarded a prize by Pete Brown, the lyricist for Cream. After an apprenticeship at the rough end of rock and roll, where he worked as a roadie, fly-poster, and t-shirt printer, he graduated into mainstream journalism and spent the 1980s working in magazine publishing. He became a freelance writer in the 1990s and has contributed to publications as diverse as *Just Seventeen* and the *Church Times*. He wrote a column for the *Guardian* for over a decade and contributes to several other newspapers, including the *Independent* and the *Express*. He has also published poetry and short stories.

He became interested in Jimi Hendrix and psychedelic London through talking to the people who were there.

about the MusicPlace series

Offering an entirely new perspective on some of the greatest names in popular music, the MusicPlace series unravels the relationships between musicians and the cities they called home. Packed with details about the musician's life and work and with stories about the city's neighborhoods and nightspots, each volume in the series captures the mood, the culture, and the sounds of a revolutionary era in popular music.

Other titles in the MusicPlace series include *Grunge Seattle* and *Bob Dylan: New York*. Roaring Forties Press also publishes the ArtPlace series and Insider's Guides.

Visit www.roaringfortiespress.com for details about our current and forthcoming titles, as well as to learn about author events, read reviews, and join our mailing list. Visitors to the website may also send comments and questions to Roaring Forties Press authors.

* * *

Cover design: Nigel Quinney and Jeff Urbancic
Interior design: Nigel Quinney
Layout: Garrett Guillotte